# BIBLE
# CODE II

# BIBLE CODE II

## THE COUNTDOWN

MICHAEL DROSNIN

VIKING

VIKING
Published by the Penguin Group
Penguin Putnam Inc., 375 Hudson Street,
New York, New York 10014, U.S.A.
Penguin Books Ltd, 80 Strand,
London WC2R 0RL, England
Penguin Books Australia Ltd, 250 Camberwell Road, Camberwell,
Victoria 3124, Australia
Penguin Books Canada Ltd, 10 Alcorn Avenue,
Toronto, Ontario, Canada M4V 3B2
Penguin Books India (P) Ltd, 11 Community Centre, Panchsheel Park,
New Delhi – 110 017, India
Penguin Books (N.Z.) Ltd, Cnr Rosedale and Airborne Roads, Albany,
Auckland, New Zealand
Penguin Books (South Africa) (Pty) Ltd, 24 Sturdee Avenue,
Rosebank, Johannesburg 2196, South Africa

Penguin Books Ltd, Registered Offices:
Harmondsworth, Middlesex, England

First published in 2002 by Viking Penguin,
a member of Penguin Putnam Inc.

Maps on pages 40 and 47 created by Compass Projections;
adapted for use in this work.

CIP data available

ISBN 0-670-03210-7

Printed in the United States of America
Set in New Aster

*For my family,*
*For my friends,*
*For all who kept the faith,*
*Again.*

*And there shall be a time of trouble,*
*such as never was since there was a nation.*
—BOOK OF DANIEL 12:1

*To solve any problem that has never been solved before,*
*you have to leave the door to the unknown ajar.*
—RICHARD FEYNMAN,
NOBEL LAUREATE PHYSICIST

# CONTENTS

# INTRODUCTION

For 3000 years a code in the Bible has remained hidden. Now it has been unlocked by computer, and it may reveal our future.

Five years ago I published a book about the discovery of the Bible code by a famous Israeli mathematician.

That book made the Bible code known throughout the world, and I hoped that my small role in this adventure was over. I'm a reporter, not a prophet, not a scientist, not a Bible scholar.

And the Bible code has always remained a puzzle to me. I am not religious, and I do not believe in God, so I cannot even imagine how there could be a code in the Bible that reveals events that happened after the Bible was written.

But I am certain that the Bible code is real.

I have seen predictions in the code come true, again and again. I even warned a Prime Minister that the code said he would be assassinated, and then watched in horror when he was killed, as the code predicted, in the year the code predicted.

September 11, 2001 was foreseen, in a text that is 3000 years old.

I met with great scientists in the United States and Israel, and I confirmed the Bible code with a senior code-breaker at the U.S. National Security Agency, the spy agency that makes and breaks codes for American military intelligence.

I learned Hebrew, and worked with an Israeli translator to confirm every code finding.

I met often and talked weekly with the mathematician who discovered the code, Dr. Eliyahu Rips, one of the world's leading experts in group theory, the field of math that underlies quantum physics.

I confirmed the mathematical significance of every major encoding with Dr. Rips, in addition to checking the odds calculated by the computer program he developed with his colleague Dr. Alexander Rotenberg.

I heard the clamor of critics who challenged Rips. I even hoped that one of them might find proof that the code was not real—it would free me of a terrible responsibility I did not want, and did not feel equal to.

But no critic found any evidence that the Bible code was not real, and indeed the evidence that there was a code in the Bible that revealed the future kept getting stronger (see Appendix).

Finally, three things forced me to continue my quest—September 11, brutal proof that the warnings encoded in the Bible were all too real; the spiral of violence in the Middle East that threatened to engulf the entire world in war; and a startling discovery that might lead to the ultimate truth behind the Bible code.

This book begins a search for the key that may unlock the code completely, reveal our forgotten past, and our entire future.

And now the search has become urgent. Because the Bible code warns that we may have only four years to survive.

# BIBLE
# CODE II

CHAPTER ONE

## END OF DAYS

At 8:48 A.M. on September 11, 2001 I was awakened by the sound of an explosion that changed the world forever.

I turned on my clock radio and heard a news bulletin—a jumbo jet had crashed into one of the World Trade Center towers.

I ran up to my roof just in time to see a second Boeing 767 fly right into the second of the Twin Towers, setting it ablaze. It was obviously no accident. The two planes had been hijacked by terrorists. New York was under attack.

For more than an hour I stood alone on my roof and watched with increasing horror and disbelief as those two 110-story buildings, the silver monoliths that loomed over Lower Manhattan where I live, continued to burn, shooting giant orange flames out of the gaping holes, spewing huge plumes of black smoke up into the sky.

Suddenly, one of the towers collapsed. It just fell straight down. And then the second tower also imploded. They both disappeared in a cloud of dust that rushed up the street right toward me. In an instant they were gone.

My mind could not take in the scale of the destruction my eyes had seen. It was on a scale only captured in Biblical prophecy.

I ran down from the roof and immediately searched the ancient code on my computer, the Bible code. It was the one place I might find confirmation of the full danger, and a revelation of what was yet to come.

The hidden code, discovered in the Bible by a famous Israeli mathematician, had already revealed other world-shaking events that took place thousands of years after the Bible was written.

Now it revealed the entire event I had just witnessed. What I watched from my roof only minutes earlier, was there in detail on my computer screen in ancient Hebrew characters.

"Twin Towers" was encoded in the 3000-year-old text. "Airplane" appeared in exactly the same place. "It caused to fall, knocked down" crossed "airplane" and "towers."

What I saw happen with my own eyes on September 11, 2001 was encoded in the Bible 3000 years ago.

○ TWIN ◇ TOWERS □ AIRPLANE

As I watched it all happen, I had only one thought, and when the first tower fell I said it out loud—"Oh my God, it's real."

○ TWIN  ◇ TOWERS  ▽ IT KNOCKED DOWN  ☐ TWICE  ◇ AIRPLANE

It was not this terrorist attack that really shook me. It was what the Bible code predicted was yet to come.

It had already predicted the assassinations of John F. Kennedy and Yitzhak Rabin. Everything from World War II to Watergate, from the Holocaust to Hiroshima, from the Moon landing to the Gulf War, had been foreseen. Sometimes the predictions were found in advance, and the events happened exactly as predicted.

And now every detail of September 11 was there, too. Suddenly, brutally, I had absolute proof that the Bible code was real.

So when the planes slammed into the towers, as I watched the horror begin to unfold, I also saw visions of a future too terrible to imagine, but clearly foretold in the code. And suddenly, it all seemed totally plausible.

For five years I had been warning world leaders that an ancient prophecy was about to come true, that the Apocalypse foretold by all the West's three major religions was encoded in the Bible, that we might face the real Armageddon—a nuclear World War starting with an act of terrorism in the Middle East—within a decade. But I could not fully believe it myself.

President Clinton had my book with him at Camp David, and my letter warning him that we faced a war in the Holy Land that could engulf the entire world.

"I hesitate to state it in detail, because it sounds so Apocalyptic," I told Clinton, holding something back even as I warned him. I could not bring myself to tell the President the world might come to an end.

Yet just within the past year I had finally told the President of the United States, the Prime Minister of Israel, and the leader of the Palestinians that according to the Bible code we were already in the ultimate time of danger, the End of Days.

I had sat with Yasir Arafat in his embattled headquarters in Ramallah, and with Shimon Peres in Tel Aviv, and with Ariel Sharon's son in Jerusalem, and with Bill Clinton's Chief of Staff in the White House, and told them all that we might have only five years left to save the world.

But no one would heed the warning.

Just the day before the September 11 attack I had talked to the White House again to see if the new President, George W. Bush, had received a letter I sent him, warning that we might face World War III while he was in office.

My letter to Bush, sent more than a month before Arab terrorists struck New York and Washington, stated:

"Now the Bible code warns that the world may face its ultimate danger—a nuclear World War starting in the Middle East—while you are in office.

"This critical moment was without doubt clearly foreseen.

"'Bush,' 'Arafat,' and 'Sharon' are all encoded together by name in the Bible with the time of danger long foretold by all three major Western religions—the 'End of Days.'

"And the Bible code clearly states the danger in modern terms— 'atomic holocaust' and 'World War' are both encoded in the Bible. And both are encoded with the same year, 2006."

On September 11 the President himself said that we were at war, that the "first war of the twenty-first century has begun." And a column in the *New York Times* was headlined "WORLD WAR III."

But until September 11 I never entirely believed it myself. I am not religious. I don't believe in God. I'm a secular, skeptical investigative reporter. I started out on the night police beat at the *Washington Post*, I covered corporate news at the *Wall Street Journal*, and I still have a flat-footed sense of reality. So although I wrote a book that made the Bible code known to the world, I woke up every morning doubting the danger was real.

On the morning of September 11 I was awakened by the event that proved it real.

Suddenly there was no room for doubt. It wasn't just Israel, it was the United States, it was New York. It was the city where I lived. It was just down the block. And I saw it happen with my own eyes.

The attack on New York, the attack on the World Trade Center, this unbelievable horror was not only encoded in the Bible—I had actually seen it in advance.

I had found it in 1993, right after the failed terrorist attack on the same two towers. "Twin Towers" was encoded in the Bible with "the warning, the slaughter," and that was crossed by "terror." "Terror" appeared a second time, and "it will fall, collapse" was also encoded twice.

But I assumed it was about the past, not the future. It never occurred to me that lightning would strike twice—that there would be another terrorist attack on the same two monoliths eight years later, that it would succeed, and knock both towers down.

And I never thought to look in the code for "airplane." As I explained to a friend at the CIA later that day, "No one could have imagined it would be done that way." "Someone did," he said.

After it happened, the warning was clear. It had been hidden in the Bible for 3000 years. Now it was obvious. Every detail was there.

The scientist who discovered the Bible code, Eliyahu Rips, found the same extraordinary code table on September 11 at his home in Jerusalem, and e-mailed it to me from Israel.

When I spoke to Dr. Rips, one of the world's leading authorities in group theory, a field of math that underlies quantum physics, he told me that he had calculated the odds.

The odds against the three key words—"twin" and "towers" and "airplane"—all appearing together in exactly the same place in the Bible, the odds against it happening by chance, were at least 10,000 to 1.

There was more. Osama bin Laden was named in the Bible code. Rips had found a single code sequence that declared him guilty—"the sin, the crime of bin Laden"—and it appeared in Genesis where the plain text told of "the city and the tower."

Also, in the same place, the original words of the Bible stated, "They saw the smoke rising above the land like the smoke of a furnace."

○ SIN, CRIME OF BIN LADEN     ◇    THE CITY AND THE TOWER
□ THEY SAW SMOKE RISING ABOVE THE LAND LIKE THE SMOKE OF A FURNACE

The leader of the hijackers, the pilot of the first plane that hit the towers, Mohammed Atta, was also identified.

O TERRORIST ATTA   □ EGYPTIAN MAN

"Terrorist Atta" was encoded in the Bible, and "Egyptian man" appeared in the same place.

There was another target, the headquarters of the American military in Washington. The Pentagon was struck by a third hijacked plane an hour after the first attack in New York. That, too, was encoded.

"Pentagon" appeared once in the Bible, crossed by "damaged." Again, the prediction in the 3000 year old text was exact. One of the five sides of the Pentagon had fallen, but the building itself still stood.

"Emergency" appeared with "Pentagon," immediately followed by "from Arabia." In fact, it was learned in the next few days that most of the terrorists had come from Saudi Arabia.

◇ PENTAGON □ DAMAGED ◇ EMERGENCY FROM ARABIA

The warning of the greatest terrorist attack in the history of the world, of the first foreign attack on mainland America in modern times, had been encoded in the Bible for 3000 years. But we had missed it, until it was too late.

And now the code warned that it would lead to war. "The next war" crossed the Hebrew name for the World Trade Towers, "the Twins." "Terrorist" was encoded in the same place.

○ THE NEXT WAR □ THE TWINS ◇ TERRORIST

The statement in the code was chilling. This terrorist attack was the start of a new war, the war that Bush declared, a war against terrorism that many were predicting would last years.

And now I saw the encoding that captured the full horror of this moment. "Towers" and "the Twins" again appeared together in exactly the same place as the words in the plain text of the Bible that again made clear that the final countdown had begun—"in the End of Days."

ת י ש ע ו ו ס ת ה ש ה ו י צ ר א ב ס ת נ ש ו נ ו ס י נ ב י נ ב ו ס
ר א ה ל ע מ ר ה מ ו י ד ב א ת ד ב א י כ צ ר א ⬦א̇⬦א̇⬦ן̇⬦ס̇⬦ ⬦ב̇ ש
ב ר פ מ ס מ י ת מ ס ת ר א ש ו ו ס י מ ע ב ס כ ת א • ו ה י צ י פ
ו ן ח י ר י א ל י נ נ ל כ א י א ל ו נ ו ע מ ש י א ל ו נ ו א ר
י ד ע ת ב ש ו ⟦ס⟧⟦י⟧⟦מ⟧⟦י⟧⟦ה⟧⟦ת⟧⟦י⟧⟦ו⟧⟦ת⟧⟦א⟧⟦ב⟧ ה ל א מ ס י ר ב ה ל כ ד
י מ י ל א נ ל א ש י כ ⓢ ה ל ש ב ש נ ר ש א ד י ת ב א ת י ב ת
נ ה ו א ה ז ה ל ו ד ג ה ר ב ד כ ה י ה נ ה ס י מ ש ה ה צ ק ד ע
ב ו ת ת א ב ת ס מ ב י ו ⓐ ב ר ק מ י ו ג ו ל ח ת ק ל א ו ב ס ו
ד ל ת א ה ה ת א ד י י ע ל ס י צ מ ב ס כ י • ל א • ו ה י
ה ד ו ת מ ת ע מ ש ו י י ר ב ⓦ ו ה ל י ד ג ה ו ש א ת א ד א ר ה צ
ל ד י נ פ מ ד מ מ ס י מ צ י ו ס י ל ד ת ס י י ג ש י י ה ה ס
ד ו ע ן י א ת ח ה מ צ ר א ה ⓛ ע ו י ע מ מ ס י מ ש ב ס י ה ל א
ד י • ל א • ו ה י ר ש א ה מ ד א ה ל ע ס מ י מ י ד י ר א ת ו ע מ
מ ו ל א נ ש א ל א ו ה ו ת ע ד ⓘ ל ב ב ו ה ל ע ה ת א ח צ ר ו ש
ז ו י ש נ מ ל ו ש ב ב ן ל ו י ג ת א ו י ד ר ל ד ג ל ב ג מ מ א ר
ב ו ד ר י ה ר ב ע ב ס ו ר צ מ מ ⓢ ת א צ ב ל א ר ש י • נ ב ל א
ר א ת א ו ו צ ר א ת א ו י ש ר י י ו ס י צ מ ס ת א צ ב ל א ר

◇ TWIN   ○ TOWERS   □ IN THE END OF DAYS

For years I had been warning top government leaders in Washington and in the Middle East that the world might be facing danger on a scale only captured in Biblical prophecy, and now I had seen the reality begin to unfold with my own eyes, just down the block from my home in New York.

And I was certain that this was the beginning of something too horrible for any of us to fully imagine, not the end.

---

"A cryptogram set by the Almighty," the "riddle of the Godhead, the riddle of past and future events divinely fore-ordained."

That's what Sir Isaac Newton called the Bible code. Three hundred years ago Newton, the first modern scientist, the man who discovered gravity and figured out the mechanics of our solar system, who single-handedly invented advanced mathematics, searched for a hidden code in the Bible that would reveal the future of mankind.

For more than 3000 years, ever since there's been a Bible, people have believed there was something hidden in it, great secrets that were known only to the high priests, new revelations that could be found using some esoteric formula, some form of magic, some new science.

But it remained for a Russian immigrant to Israel, Eliyahu Rips, a mathematician freed from a Soviet political prison, to find the code that had eluded everyone for millennia.

Rips succeeded because he had the one essential tool that everyone before him lacked—a computer.

The Bible code had a time lock. It could not be opened until the computer was invented.

It was designed, apparently by some intelligence that could see the future, to be opened now. That much seemed clear. The code could have been designed to be found by Newton 300 years ago. Or it could have been designed to be found 300 or 3000 years in the future, by a technology that would not exist until then.

Instead, some intelligence that could see across time encoded the Bible in a way that allowed us to crack the code at this one moment in human history.

"That is why Isaac Newton could not do it," said Rips. "It had to be opened with a computer. It was 'sealed until the time of the End.'"

But when Eli Rips began his search for the Bible code nearly twenty years ago, he was not thinking about the "End of Days."

He was just solving a mathematical puzzle. "I found words encoded far more than statistics allowed for by random chance, and I knew that I was on to something of real importance," recalled Rips. "When I applied a computer, I made the breakthrough."

Rips discovered the Bible code in the original Hebrew version of the Old Testament, the Bible as it was first written, the words that according to the Bible itself God gave to Moses on Mount Sinai 3200 years ago.

Rips eliminated all the spaces between the words, and turned the entire original Bible into one continuous letter strand, 304,805 letters long.

In doing that, he was actually restoring the Bible to what ancient sages say was its original form. According to legend, it was the way Moses received the Bible from God—"contiguous, without break of words."

Rips wrote a computer program that searched the strand of letters for new information revealed by skipping any equal number of letters.

Anyone could make up a sentence that would tell one story on the surface, but another story hidden in a simple skip code. For example:

Rips explained that each code is a case of adding every fifth or tenth or fiftieth letter to form a word.

Now read that same sentence as a four-letter skip code:

**R**ips Expl**A**ine**D** tha**T** eac**H** cod**E** is a **C**ase **O**f ad**D**ing **E**very fifth or tenth or fiftieth letter to form a word.

The hidden message—**READ THE CODE.**

But no one, not even Newton, could go through the whole Bible counting letters by hand, checking every possible skip sequence, starting with every letter from the first verse to the last verse, backwards and forwards, from the beginning of the Bible to the end. Only a computer can search fast enough to make the job possible.

And only a computer could find the complexly interwoven information in the Bible code. Time after time related words, names, dates, and places are, against all odds, encoded together.

The words form a crossword puzzle. Each time a new word or phrase is discovered, a new crossword puzzle is created. And the connected words reveal accurate, often detailed information about modern events.

It's what makes the Bible code unique. In another book one might find a random skip sequence that spells "Twin Towers"—but not with "airplane." One might find "bin Laden"—but not with "the city and the tower." One might find "the Twins"—but not with "the next war," or "the End of Days."

"Only in the Bible code is there consistent, coherent information," said Rips. "No one has found anything like that in any other book, in any translation, or in any original Hebrew text, except the Bible."

When Rips reported his discovery in an American mathematics journal, many scientists were skeptical. They couldn't fault his science, but they couldn't believe his results. The claim was just too amazing—a code in the Bible that revealed events that happened after the Bible was written.

A senior code-breaker at the top secret National Security Agency, the clandestine U.S. government listening post near Washington, heard about the startling claim, and decided to investigate.

Harold Gans had spent his life making and breaking codes for American military intelligence, and he was sure the Bible code was "off-the-wall, ridiculous."

He wrote his own computer program, and set out to prove it was a hoax. Instead, he replicated the results of Rips's experiment. The names of 66 sages who lived and died long after Biblical times were indeed encoded with the dates they were born, and the dates that they died. Gans could not believe it. He thought that the experiment must have been rigged. He looked for new information, encodings that Rips never tried to find. He was sure that the names of the cities where the 66 rabbis lived and died could not be found in the code. He found them.

Gans had set out to debunk the Bible code. Instead, his 440-hour experiment proved it was real.

"It sent a chill up my spine," recalled the code-breaker.

No man could have encoded the Bible with information about people who lived, events that happened, thousands of years after the Bible was written. But someone did.

If not one of us, then who?

————————————————

I first heard about the Bible code ten years ago. I had just met with the chief of Israeli intelligence to discuss the future of warfare. As I was leaving intelligence headquarters, a young officer I'd met stopped me.

"There's a mathematician in Jerusalem you should see," he said. "He found the exact date the Gulf War would begin. In the Bible."

"I'm not religious," I said, getting into my car.

"Neither am I," said the officer. "But he found a code in the Bible with the exact date, three weeks before the war started."

It all seemed beyond belief. I was sure it was crazy. But when I checked Rips out, I found that he was considered a near genius in the world of mathematics. I went to see him.

With his full beard and yarmulka Eliyahu Rips looked like a character straight out of the Old Testament. It confirmed all my doubts. Genius or not, this scientist was surely deluded by his religious beliefs. I challenged him to show me the Gulf War in his Bible. Instead, he led me into his small study, and showed me a prediction of the Gulf War encoded on his computer screen.

"Saddam Hussein" and "Scud missiles" were encoded in the Bible with the exact day Iraq attacked Israel, January 18, 1991.

"How many dates did you find?" I asked.

"Just this one, three weeks before the war started," he replied.

But I was still skeptical. I asked Rips to look for modern events he had not already found.

We found "President Kennedy" with "Dallas." We found "Bill Clinton" with "President"—six months before he was elected. We found one thing after another encoded in the Bible, things that Rips did not know I would ask him. Eventually, we found several events before they happened—including the collision of a comet with the planet Jupiter, with the name of the comet, and the exact date of impact.

The Bible code kept coming true. A top American code-breaker had confirmed it. Famous mathematicians in Israel and in the United States, at Harvard, and Yale, and Hebrew University, said it was real.

Rips's experiment passed three peer reviews at a respected U.S. mathematics journal. But still I could not believe it.

And then, finally, two years later, I found an encoding that persuaded even me.

On September 1, 1994, I flew back to Israel and met in Jerusalem with a close friend of Prime Minister Yitzhak Rabin, the poet Chaim Guri. I gave him a letter, which he immediately gave to the Prime Minister.

"I have uncovered information that suggests your life is in danger," my letter to Rabin stated. "The only time your full name—Yitzhak Rabin—is encoded in the Bible, the words 'assassin that will assassinate' cross your name."

O YITZHAK RABIN    □ ASSASSIN THAT WILL ASSASSINATE

A year later, on November 4, 1995, came the awful confirmation—a shot in the back from a man who believed he was on a mission from God, the murder that was encoded in the Bible 3000 years ago.

When I heard the news, all the air went out of me. I sank to the floor, and spoke the same words I said out loud when the World Trade Towers fell—"Oh my God, it's real."

The shock was not that Rabin was dead. It was that the Bible code was real.

But as great as the shock was on November 4, 1995, it was yet greater on September 11, 2001. Because now I knew what else the code predicted.

If the Bible code was real, and I could no longer doubt it, it could have only one purpose—to warn the world of a terrible, even terminal danger. And the danger must be right upon us, or we would not be finding the Bible code now. Perhaps we really were, right now, facing the "End of Days."

---

The two great Biblical Apocalypses, the Book of Daniel in the Old Testament and the Book of Revelation in the New Testament, are predictions of unprecedented horror, to be fully revealed when a secret sealed book is opened at the "End of Days."

The End is foretold four times in the original five books of the Bible, the words that God dictated to Moses, what Jews call the Torah. It is predicted again in Daniel. An angel reveals the ultimate future to the ancient prophet, and then tells him, "But thou, O Daniel, shut up the words, and seal the book until the time of the End."

There are two ways to write the "End of Days" in Hebrew, and they appear together only once in the Bible.

"In the End of Days" appears in the original text of Deuteronomy, in words spoken by Moses to the ancient Israelites wandering in the desert. In the table below, that appears horizontally.

י ח ה נ פ י ל כ ב ב ו ן נ ו ו נ נ ב ע ש ו ה י י ו י י ו ה י י נ פ ל
ו ב ק י ת א ו ב ת כ ו י ו ן ר ג ת א ו ב ת כ ס י ו ל ל ב ל ב ש ח נ ו ו
מ ב ש ח ת י א ל ס י ו ג ו ן כ ש י ד ד ב ל ס ע ו ן ה י י ר ו ש
ס ו ו ן מ ש ב ה ל ו ל ב ה ח נ מ ת ל ס ס ו י (נ) ר ש ע י נ ש ו מ ס מ ח
י ה ר ל א ר ש י מ ו • י ה י מ ס י ק נ ס ה (י) י ה י י ב ש ה ר ח
א ה ס ת ו א ן ה א י ס י ע ד י י ס י מ כ ח (ה) י ו נ א ס כ י ט ב
ע ת ב ש ו │ס י מ י ה ת י ו ה ח א ב│ ה ל א ה ס (ו) ר ב ד ה ל כ ד י א
כ ש ת ל ה מ כ ז ה ת א ף ר ע ה ש ק ס ע י כ (ה) ת ש ר ל ת א ז ה ה
א ר ש י ל כ ו ס י ד ע ת ה י ב מ ס י ר צ מ (ר) א מ ד א י צ ו מ
ן ת נ ז י • ל א • ו ה י ר ש א ד צ ר א ב ר (ק) ב י י ק נ ס ד ך פ ש
ח ו ס י נ ק ז ה י נ י ע ל ו י ל א ו ת מ ב י ה ש ג נ ו ה ה נ ח ק
ת ב א ל ע ב ש ו ר י ש א כ ו ד ל ב ד ר ש א ס י ה ל א ל ד ל ה
ו ר ש ו י כ ב ו י ח א ר י י ז נ ד ק ד ק ל ו ף ס ו י ש א ר ל ה ת

○ END OF DAYS   □ IN THE END OF DAYS

The other statement of the "End of Days" that appears vertically are the words of Daniel, but encoded in the Torah, exactly where Moses warns of a future time of terrible danger.

The odds against those two phrases appearing together in the Bible are at least 100 to 1.

But there was more.

Right after the Fourth of July in 2000, President Clinton announced that Israeli Prime Minister Ehud Barak and the Palestinian leader Yasir Arafat would meet with him at Camp David for peace talks. Everyone knew the stakes were high, but not even the three leaders could have fully imagined the magnitude of the moment revealed by the Bible code.

In the only place that the two Biblical expressions of the "End of Days" are encoded together, "Arafat" appears with no skips, perfectly spelled in the plain text of the Bible right below "in the End of Days."

And "E. Barak," again perfectly spelled with no skips, crosses the second code statement of the "End of Days."

I had shown that code table to Eli Rips more than two years earlier, in

○ END OF DAYS    □ IN THE END OF DAYS    ◇ ARAFAT    ▽ E. BARAK

1998, a full year before Barak was elected Prime Minister. But even when that prediction came true and Barak became Israel's new leader, Rips was more focused on Arafat. "Arafat is old, and he's ill," said Rips. "If he's involved, then we are already in the End of Days."

Rips calculated the odds that the names of the leaders of the Israelis and the Palestinians would appear together in exactly the place that "in the End of Days" was encoded with "End of Days." The odds against it happening by chance were at least 150,000 to 1.

So when Clinton announced the summit meeting, I immediately sent him a letter: "I've enclosed a copy of my book *The Bible Code,* because your announcement today of a Camp David summit meeting between Barak and Arafat confirms what the code foretold."

"The stakes are even higher than you may imagine," my letter continued. "The alternative is starkly stated in the Bible code, the real Armageddon, a nuclear world war starting in the Middle East."

When Camp David ended in failure, and a new Intifada began, when the right-wing general Ariel Sharon, an outspoken opponent of the peace plan, became the new Prime Minister of Israel, and George W. Bush became the new President of the United States, it again confirmed what the Bible code predicted.

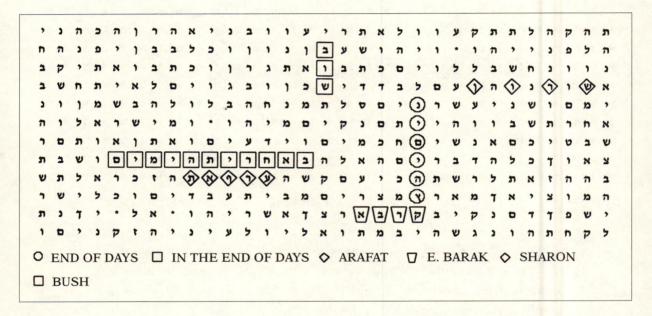

O END OF DAYS  □ IN THE END OF DAYS  ◇ ARAFAT  ▽ E. BARAK  ◇ SHARON
□ BUSH

Not only were both elections foreseen, but both "Bush" and "Sharon" were encoded in the Bible, with "Arafat" and "Barak," where "End of Days" was encoded with "in the End of Days."

Dr. Rips was amazed. He again checked the odds. The odds against the names of all four leaders—of Israel, and the Palestinians, and the United States—all appearing together with the two Biblical expressions of the "End of Days" were at least 500,000 to 1. Rips said the true odds might be 1 million to 1, but it was impossible to fully calculate such a complex series of matches.

"In any event, it is far beyond chance," said Rips. "It is obviously intentional. It is mathematically certain. It's a perfect table. And it is clearly about this moment in time."

Yet it had all been there for more than 3000 years, the names of today's world leaders encoded with the ancient prophecy, waiting for us to find it at the moment we needed to hear the warning.

The Bible code clearly, without question, against overwhelming odds, stated that we were right now living in that long-foreseen time of ultimate danger.

The End of Days, the Apocalypse, was no longer some religious myth, some frightening vision of a nightmare that would never really happen, just words in an ancient text. It was no longer something long ago or far away.

It was right here, right now.

---

Four years ago, in October 1998, I gave my lawyer, Michael Kennedy, a prominent New York attorney, a sealed letter to be opened in 2002. The letter stated:

"Michael:

"I'm convinced of two things:

"(1) The Bible code is real;

"(2) The world won't listen to its warnings until it's almost too late."

It was that way the last time the whole world was in danger. No one wanted to confront Hitler. America almost lost World War II, because we entered it years too late. Now I was trying to warn the world of a yet greater danger, and the source of the warning was even to me bizarre—a code in the Bible.

"The code challenges all conventional Western concepts of reality," the sealed letter continued. "So, although Newton believed that the future could be known and that a code in the Bible would reveal it, and a top NSA code breaker has confirmed the Israeli discovery, it still isn't fully accepted.

"Even the fact that the code has been right in advance about the Rabin assassination, the Gulf War, and other major world events, has not convinced the skeptics.

"Prime Minister Peres and the chief of the Mossad met with me, but most government leaders will not heed the warnings until more predictions come true.

"Therefore, I've put the most important in writing, so I can prove that these predictions were found in advance.

"The warnings that are most clearly stated in the code are:

"(a) the world will face global 'economic collapse' starting in the Hebrew year 5762, (2002 in the modern calendar);

"(b) this will lead to a period of unprecedented danger, as nations with nuclear weapons become unstable, and terrorists can buy or steal the power to destroy whole cities;

"(c) the danger will peak in the Hebrew year 5766 (2006 in the modern calendar), the year that is most clearly encoded with both 'world war' and 'atomic holocaust.'"

On September 11, 2001, after I had seen the attack on the World Trade Towers, after I found it perfectly encoded in the Bible, I retrieved my copy of that sealed letter.

When I read it, it shook me.

The fall of the very symbol of our economic power, the World Trade Center, and the attack on the very symbol of our military power, the Pentagon, made the predicted dangers look all too real.

On September 17, the eve of the Hebrew New Year 5762 that was encoded with "economic crisis," the stock markets reopened for the first time since September 11. The Dow Jones fell 684 points, its biggest loss in history, beginning a week that saw the worst stock market crash since 1929, since the Great Depression.

The first Bible code prediction had already been fulfilled.

My fear was that a new depression could lead to a third World War, just as the economic collapse of the 1930s led to the rise of Hitler and World War II.

"World War," and "atomic holocaust," and "End of Days" are all encoded with "in 5766," the Hebrew year equivalent to 2006.

I checked every year in the next hundred, and only 2006 appeared with all three warnings. It was a clear prediction that we might face World War III in just five years.

I told Dr. Rips. He calculated the odds on the big computer at Hebrew University. He checked a hundred thousand random texts to see if all the greatest dangers might appear by chance with the same year in any place other than the Bible.

"It's 100,000 to 1," Rips reported. "I looked in 100,000 random texts, and these words appear together only in the Bible. It could not be by chance. Someone intentionally put this warning into the Torah."

It was beyond any doubt. A hundred to one is the normal test. A thousand to one is the strictest standard ever applied by mathematicians. A hundred thousand to one is decisive.

According to the Bible code, we might really face the ultimate danger, a nuclear World War, in 2006.

○ WORLD WAR   ☐ IN 5766/2006

World War II ended with an atomic bomb. World War III might begin with one. There are now at least 50,000 nuclear weapons spread throughout the world, from atomic artillery shells and suitcase bombs, to multi-warhead intercontinental ballistic missiles, each more powerful than the Hiroshima bomb.

"Atomic holocaust" is encoded with 1945, the year the bomb was dropped on Hiroshima, and with 2006.

○ ATOMIC HOLOCAUST    □ IN 5766/2006

If the Bible code is right, World War III—a war that will be fought with weapons of mass destruction the world has never seen used in battle before—might happen within just a few years. The whole world could be obliterated within a few hours. It would literally be the End of Days.

But instead of a nuclear war between superpowers, the conflict everyone dreaded all through the Cold War, the world might now face a new threat—terrorists armed with nuclear weapons.

"Terrorism" is encoded with "World War," and the Arabic word for suicide bomber, "Shahid," appears in exactly the same place. So does "war to the knife."

Apocalyptic religious fanatics, terrorists armed with weapons of mass destruction, men who believe they are on a mission from God, they are the ultimate danger encoded in the Bible.

○ WORLD WAR   ○ TERRORISM   ◇ SUICIDE BOMBER   □ WAR TO THE KNIFE

What happened on September 11 may have been the beginning, not the end.

But the sealed letter I gave my lawyer in 1998 left room for hope, and I still, even after September 11, 2001 remained an optimist. The letter went on to say:

"But the Bible code tells us all our possible futures, not one predetermined future. So we can change course, prevent the ultimate disaster.

"I believe the Bible code exists to help us prevent it. I believe that the code was discovered now, at this moment in human history, so that we would know just in time.

"That's why I've left this time capsule with you, sealed in 1998, to be opened in 2002, to prepare us for 2006."

But by the time I wrote that sealed letter, I had already begun to search for another message, sealed in some distant time past, the sealed message we might have to find now if we were to survive.

# CHAPTER TWO

# CODE KEY

In the predawn darkness of the desert, the ground suddenly began to shake, and there was a terrible thunder, and the people came running out of their tents and stared up in terror at the mountain that towered over them, its peak now illuminated by a bright white light, as if the mountain itself was on fire.

Suddenly a voice from out of nowhere said, "Moses, come up to me to the mountain. "

It was 1200 B.C. Moses went up to the top of Mount Sinai.

And according to the plain text of the Bible, he "saw the God of Israel, and there was under his feet a kind of paved work of Sapphire stone."

According to legend it was on that "Sapphire stone" that God wrote the original words of the Bible. Although the stone was as hard as a diamond, it could be rolled up like a scroll. And although it was the deepest deep blue, it was also transparent. In fact, the Bible said it was "the very Heaven for clearness."

One night, alone in my loft in New York, I read that passage in the Bible and for the first time realized that the words of the Bible were first written on "Sapphire."

I immediately wondered whether in that obscure detail was the secret to the Bible code.

If there really was a code in the Bible that revealed the future, I thought, it must itself be foretold in the story of God giving the Bible to Moses on Mount Sinai, engraving the words on Sapphire.

I examined the text over and over again. There was a hint, a clue. In Hebrew the word for "book" is "Sefer." It is spelled with the same three letters as "Sapphire," perhaps because the first book, the Bible, was written on that stone.

Then I saw that "Sapphire" also means "countable"—perhaps suggesting that there was from the beginning a mathematical code in the Bible. I searched for a complex number scheme. But I made no breakthrough.

Suddenly, I saw something very simple. In Hebrew, the original language of the Bible, "Sapphire" in reverse spells "Rips."

ספיר = ריפס

**Sapphire = Rips**

Eliyahu Rips, the mathematician who discovered the Bible code, appeared by name in the Bible, in the place that the Bible tells the story of God coming down on Mount Sinai.

I was shocked. Dr. Rips was himself foreseen in the code that he discovered, the code in the Bible that revealed the future.

The very name "Sapphire," the deep blue gemstone on which the Bible was originally written, foretold the scientist who would find the code three thousand years later.

It was clearly no accident that "Sapphire" read backwards spelled "Rips." Mirror writing is a very ancient tradition. Indeed, the Bible itself says it is the way to see the future. The first of the prophets, Isaiah, said it: "To see the future you must look backwards." The same Hebrew words can be translated, "Read the letters in reverse."

There could be no doubt about it. Not only was Rips named in the mirror writing, his deed was also clearly stated.

"Sapphire stone" reversed spells "Rips prophesied."

---

אבן ספיר = ריפס נבא

**Sapphire Stone = Rips Prophesied**

---

I flew back to Israel to see Eli Rips. It was the first time we had met in the year since my first book was published, and the Bible code had become known throughout the world, making both of us the center of a global controversy.

Was there really a code in the Bible that told the future? Had we really found the first proof that we are not alone? Was this a new revelation? Did it prove the existence of God?

I had wanted to escape it all. I am not religious, and I do not believe in God. And the Bible code seemed to predict terrible dangers, perhaps the real Apocalypse, a cataclysmic end of this world. I didn't want to believe that, either.

But now, suddenly, I had new proof that the Bible code was real. Proof I could not ignore. The man who discovered it was named in the very place that God gave the Bible to Moses, in the only verse of the Bible where God is actually seen.

And if the code was real, then the dangers it predicted must also be real. I had to go see the scientist who found the code, and who was foreseen in it, the man who might be able to help stop the countdown to Armageddon.

In 1998, just before Shavuot, the holiday that celebrates the moment in 1200 B.C. when God came down on Mount Sinai, I showed Eli Rips his name in that verse of the Bible.

Rips was not surprised. He remained as he always was, humble.

"It is no less striking than other aspects of the code," Rips said. "If detailed knowledge of the entire world is contained in it, then knowledge of each of us, and of our interaction with it, was also foreseen."

Rips took a volume down from his bookshelf, and again read to me the words he had read when we first met, quoting an eighteenth-century sage called the Genius of Vilna: "The rule is that all that was, is, and will be unto the End of time is included in the Torah, from the first word to the last word. And not merely in a general sense, but as to the details of every species and each one individually, and details of details of everything that happened to him from the day of his birth until his end."

But Rips denied that he was a prophet. "The Bible states clearly that a prophet receives his information directly from God," said the mathematician.

Although I don't believe in God, there is an aura about Rips that compelled me to ask him a question—"Is it possible that the Bible code is exactly that kind of a communication? Is it possible that God is speaking through the code directly to you?"

Rips dismissed the possibility that he was unique, and instead suggested that God and the code speak to all of us.

"You just must look for the HELP button," said Rips.

But no matter how modest Rips was, there was now no question he was named 3000 years ago in the hidden text of the Bible as the man who would discover the code.

Not only did "Sapphire stone" reversed spell "Rips prophesied," but where "Sapphire tablet" was encoded, "Russian" and "he will compute" also appeared, crossing each other.

Rips had come to Israel from Russia in 1970, when he was set free from a Soviet political prison after a worldwide protest led by the president of the American Mathematical Society.

"Rips" was the "Russian" who "computed" the code, and on the same table "he prophesied " was again encoded, crossed by "he mechanized."

But, finally, what convinced both of us was what appeared in the Bible code with "Decoder." We looked at it on his computer.

"Decoder" was crossed again by "Sapphire" and "stone"—the words that in reverse spell "Rips prophesied. " And "Code" overlapped "Decoder."

○ SAPPHIRE TABLET/RIPS ☐ RUSSIAN/HE WILL COMPUTE ◇ PROPHECY

○ DECODER ◇ RIPS ◇ PROPHESIED ☐ CODE

Rips was quiet for a moment. He examined the words on his computer. Then he spoke: "When we are used to the idea that the whole of reality is encoded, then we accept that we each have a place in the code. But seeing something this specific is much more vivid than knowing it theoretically."

"Technically, it's a very nice finding," he commented. It was typical. As always he focused on the mathematical significance, rather than on the extraordinary fact that he was clearly named in the code as the man who discovered it. Finally, Rips conceded what he had been trying to hold back. "Because I know that the Encoder is the Creator of the Universe, this is a very humbling experience," he said.

If Eliyahu Rips was not intended as the decoder of the Bible code, he was at least foreseen.

And now, in the small cramped study of his home in Jerusalem, I asked Rips if he thought we'd ever be able to see the Bible code whole.

"We don't have the key," said Rips.

"Even using the most powerful computers we possess today, we cannot solve its mystery," he continued. "I believe that the Torah is the word of God. It has everything in it. But we cannot know why, or for what purpose, until, maybe, the key to the code is found."

Rips said that the Bible code was like a giant jigsaw puzzle, and we had only a handful of the pieces. He said that God may not want us to see it whole—"the code may choose which part of the whole to reveal, to show X information to us, but not Y or Z."

"But the code says the world might come to an end in 2006," I reminded him. "We need all the pieces of the puzzle now. We have to act now, before it's too late."

"Any one piece is a part of a whole we cannot see," said Rips. "Therefore, any intervention is presumptuous."

I reminded Rips that "World War," and "atomic holocaust," and "End of Days" were all encoded with 2006, that we had checked every year in the next hundred years, and only that one year was clearly encoded—and that we were right now sitting in the one city in the world named as the target, "Jerusalem."

"We are in God's hands," Rips said.

I pressed him again. "But do you think we will ever be able to see the Bible code whole?" I asked.

"If we ever get the key, " said Rips.

———

The key. It played on my mind the whole time I was in Israel, and then one night I opened my laptop and looked in the Bible code for "Code Key." It was there four times.

Twice an obscure Hebrew word I didn't recognize crossed "Code Key." It wasn't even in my dictionary. But in the definitive Hebrew dictionary it was translated as "obelisks."

O CODE KEY   ☐ OBELISKS

Obelisks. It was not what I had expected. I had seen obelisks, tall stone pillars that came to a pyramid-shaped point. There were some 100 feet tall that still stood in Egypt. And there was one in Rome and London and Paris, each brought back from Egypt by conquerors long ago. I had even seen a 3600-year-old obelisk in New York, engraved with hieroglyphics that told the deeds of an ancient pharaoh.

But it wasn't what I had expected to find crossing "Code Key." I had imagined a mathematical formula, or a set of instructions, not a physical object, much less an obelisk.

Both times "obelisks" appeared it was as part of a phrase, "Mouth of Obelisks." It suggested that these were not merely stone pillars, but in some way oracles, that they told the future, perhaps even that they spoke.

O CODE KEY □ MOUTH OF OBELISKS

It was hard to believe. But there was no doubt that this was intentional. "Obelisks" appeared with "Code Key" twice, both times actually crossing it, two perfect matches, against all odds.

Rips started crunching the numbers on a powerful computer at Hebrew University, and e-mailed me his calculation: "'Code Key' with 'Mouth of the Obelisks' succeeds at the rate of one in a million. My congratulations!"

Later Rips told me that it was the best result he had ever seen. "No other pair has had such high statistics in the history of code research," he said. "Two direct hits could not happen by chance. It is intentional. That is mathematically certain."

And in the very same place, in the same plain text of the Bible, both times that "obelisks" crossed "Code Key" there was another phrase, "Lord of the Code."

○ CODE KEY   □ MOUTH OF OBELISKS   ◇ LORD OF CODE

Lord of the Code. In Hebrew it had yet more meaning, it could be a Biblical way of saying "the Encoder." It was too perfect.

And then I discovered that where "Lord of the Code" was encoded in the Bible it was crossed by the same verse from Exodus that told of God coming down on Mount Sinai to give Moses the Bible, written on "Sapphire," the verse that identified the scientist who discovered the code, "Rips."

And on that same table "obelisks" appeared again crossed by words in the plain text that said "an object of Heaven."

I searched for any ancient commentary that would tell me more about the "obelisks," and found in a 1700-year-old Jewish text called the Midrash immediate confirmation of the Bible code:

"What were these 'obelisks'? They were not what a human being had made, but the work of Heaven."

It was an extraordinary statement. The oldest authoritative source

○ LORD OF THE CODE    □ SAPPHIRE/RIPS    ◇ OBJECT OF HEAVEN    □ OBELISKS

clearly stated that the "obelisks" came from beyond this planet, perhaps even from another realm. But there was more. The Midrash also said they were humanoid:

"They had eyes as a window, were a kind of male and female."

The ancient text did not quite say they were alive, but it suggested they could see, and perhaps speak. And the Midrash certainly seemed to say that the obelisks were at least representative of some life form, perhaps not of this world.

I went back to see Eli Rips. He, of course, was not surprised that the obelisks were not of this world, because he was already certain that the Bible code, and the Bible itself, also came from another realm, indeed from God.

I told Rips that I had been expecting a mathematical formula, not a stone pillar, whether from this world or beyond. Rips said, "It could be both."

He told me that in Hebrew the word "key" also means "engraved." So "Code Key" can also be translated "code engraved." And that therefore it made perfect sense that the word crossing it twice was "obelisks." It suggested that the key we were seeking was engraved on stone pillars.

We looked in his computer for "mathematical key." It was also encoded. Then we both saw something extraordinary—again with "mathematical key" there appeared the same verse from Exodus that told of God coming down on Mount Sinai, the verse that said the original Bible was written on "Sapphire," the word that in reverse spelled "Rips."

We looked for "code on obelisk." It appeared once in the Bible, with "Heaven."

O CODE ON OBELISK   ☐ HEAVEN

We looked at the original encoding of "Bible code," the Bible's own confirmation of the existence of the code that we had found many years earlier. "Obelisk" crossed "Bible code."

○ BIBLE CODE    ☐ OBELISK

We were both astounded. The confirmation seemed absolute. There were, at least long ago, obelisks that held the lost secrets of the Bible code.

But if indeed there really was hard evidence of the Bible code, some physical object that might be the key we needed to see it whole, it would also of course be more than that—it would be the first hard evidence that we were not alone.

If there were in fact engraved on obelisks thousands of years old a science more advanced than we now have, a mathematical code key, then it had to come from a civilization more advanced than ours—if not from "Heaven," then at least from beyond.

No one here, no human, not thousands of years ago, not today, could have created the Bible code. Our science is still too primitive. And none of us can see across time.

So if the obelisks could be found we would not only have the key to unlock the code, and see our entire future, but we would also have proof of our hidden past.

Perhaps we would have the identity of the "Lord of the Code," the Encoder. Perhaps even the true identity of God.

But where were the obelisks ?

I was flying back to Israel just before Thanksgiving in 1998, looking at the startling encoding of "Bible code" crossed by "obelisk."

And then I saw that there was a very definite location stated in the plain text of the Bible, exactly where "obelisk" crossed "Bible code"—"in the Valley of Siddim."

O BIBLE CODE        OBELISK        □ IN THE VALLEY OF SIDDIM

I knew I had seen that place name before. I checked my laptop, and there it was—"code on obelisk" also crossed by "Valley of Siddim."

O CODE ON OBELISK   □ VALLEY OF SIDDIM

The location appeared in the plain text of the Bible, with the story of Abraham. And the full reference in Genesis 14:3 revealed where the valley was located—"the Valley of Siddim that is the Dead Sea."

The Dead Sea is, of course, well known. It lies between Israel and Jordan, an inland sea so salty that nothing can live in it.

But the Valley of Siddim did not appear on any modern map. I checked maps of Biblical sites. The Valley of Siddim still did not appear. All I could discover about the location was what was stated in Genesis. No modern scholar knew more.

Some speculated that the valley might now be underwater, not near the Dead Sea, but beneath it. One thing was clear: the Valley of Siddim was already ancient, and apparently already forgotten, when the Bible was first written more than 3000 years ago.

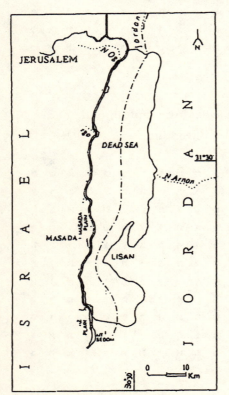

It was so ancient that when Genesis was written the location had to be identified by the sea that already covered it—before the Bible existed.

I asked rabbis and Bible scholars. The Valley of Siddim was mentioned in the Midrash, commentaries on the Bible, some 2000 years old. The most famous commentator, the Rashi, a medieval French Jew, said that the valley was once green and full of orchards, but that long ago the Mediterranean Sea flowed into it, and the Dead Sea came into existence, covering the valley.

But no ancient sage knew, and no scholar today knows, exactly where the valley once was.

I went to see the leading scientific authority on the Dead Sea area, an Israeli geologist named David Neev.

"Here is what we know from Genesis," said Neev. "The Valley is specifically described in the Bible as the Dead Sea. It is where an ancient battle was fought. It is where the kings of Sodom and Gomorrah, fleeing the battle, fell into tar pits."

Neev guessed that the Valley of Siddim must therefore be near Sodom and Gomorrah. It is his theory that a huge earthquake destroyed the two cities more than 4000 years ago, and buried them beneath the Dead Sea. That, he said, was the real event behind the myth in the Bible.

But no one knew exactly where the two doomed cities once stood. And that ancient site was almost certainly now under water.

And yet there was hope. The Dead Sea was right now at its lowest level in more than 5000 years. What had been under water since the dawn of human civilization might now again be exposed.

"The Dead Sea is like a kettle of water left on a high flame—it's just boiling away, evaporating," said Neev. "In another hundred years large parts of the sea might simply disappear. Until there's nothing left but salt."

The geologist showed me a chart that revealed the water levels. The sea had receded in the past decade to -400 meters. The last prolonged time it had been that low was between 5500 and 8000 years ago.

Was the vanishing Dead Sea about to reveal ancient secrets?

The last time it was so low was during a mysterious era when all the things that define modern civilization first arose, when seemingly out of nowhere came writing and mathematics, astronomy and agriculture, when men learned how to work metal, and cities were first built.

"If your object was erected during the Chalcolithic period, which was the sudden rise of civilization, then it's quite possible that it could have remained hidden until now," said Neev. "But if what you're looking for was built 5000 years ago, and then the sea covered it for thousands of years, when the sea recedes, you won't see an obelisk, not even a palace or an entire city, just mud and sediment and rock salt."

The geologist gave me one other clue: "'Siddim' in Hebrew means 'lime,' so I think you should be looking for a Valley of Lime. In fact, some translations of the Bible call the Valley of Siddim the 'Valley of Lime.'"

Neev suggested I look on the Jordan side of the Dead Sea. "There's a peninsula there called Lisan," he said. "It's a rock-salt dome covered by limestone."

He had never been there. Israel had fought three wars with Jordan. "Be careful," he said. "It's enemy territory."

---

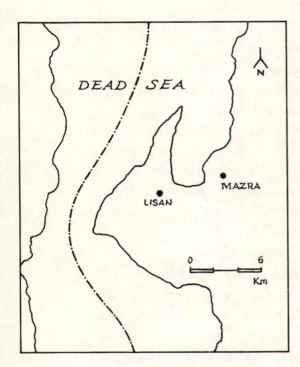

My guide did not understand why I wanted to go to the Lisan Peninsula. No tourist had ever wanted to go there before.

It is an oddly shaped landmass that juts out into the Dead Sea. It looks like a tongue, and indeed in both Hebrew and Arabic "the Lisan " means "the Tongue."

When we arrived there it was like we arrived on the dark side of the Moon. It is a totally barren moonscape, entirely devoid of any vegetation. In the bright desert sun it shone white, because it was covered entirely with lime.

It was the one place at the Dead Sea still above water that might be a remnant of the ancient "Valley of Siddim," the "Valley of Lime." It felt mythologically perfect. It is the navel of the Earth. It is the lowest place on Earth, 1300 feet below sea level.

On the entire planet there is no other dry land so low. So when I stood on the newly exposed shore of the Lisan Peninsula, the land that had been underwater just a decade ago, and had last been exposed 5000 years ago, I was standing on the lowest spot at the lowest place on Earth, at the bottom of the world.

"Bottom of the world" was encoded in the Bible. "Lisan" appeared in the same place, crossed by "ancient key."

O  BOTTOM OF WORLD          □  LISAN          ◇  ANCIENT KEY

What might have once been standing on this dry land, and was then underwater for all of the known history of human civilization, might now again be exposed, covered only by sand, and clay, and mud, and the thick salt crust that the sea left behind.

It was absolutely empty. There was not a sign of human habitation. Not now, not ever. The only other people on the entire peninsula were the workers at a salt mine.

But it was surrounded by extraordinary archaeological finds from the Biblical past.

Across the sea were the caves of Qumran where the oldest known copies of the Bible, the Dead Sea Scrolls, were found. For more than 2000 years, words handwritten on animal skin parchments had been preserved. In 1947, a shepherd boy threw a stone into one of the caves, and heard the sound of pottery breaking. Inside the broken urn he found a complete book of the Bible, untouched by time.

Also within sight, on the Israeli side of the sea, was the ancient mountaintop fortress of Masada, where 2000 years ago a small band of Jews held out against the Roman legions to the last man. On the plateau the original stones of the fortress still stood, looking out over the bleak landscape that had not changed in the two millennia gone by.

On the Jordan side, less than a mile inland from the sea, a 5000-year-old village, Bab-Edrah, had been unearthed, its ancient mud bricks still intact. It may have been the Biblical Zoar, where according to legend Lot fled to escape the destruction of Sodom and Gomorrah.

So it was not entirely implausible that perhaps buried beneath my feet, in this totally barren peninsula, there was an ancient obelisk engraved with the "Code Key."

The Lisan Peninsula was just a dot on a map, but it was twenty-five square miles, and as I stood there in the hot sun staring out over an endless vista of lime and salt, I realized it was far too big an area to search for a pillar, or even a palace, now buried beneath it, even if by chance I had stumbled onto the right place.

So I went back to the Bible, and to the code.

There is one book in the Old Testament where the Lisan is mentioned by name. It is the Book of Joshua, the story of the young warrior who led the ancient Israelites on the final journey of their exodus from Egypt, after Moses died, taking them from Jordan to Israel.

O  HE FOUND THE EXACT PLACE, LISAN
□  NORTH FROM LISAN, TONGUE OF SEA, FROM EDGE OF THE JORDAN ON THE BORDER

"Lisan, tongue of sea" appears in Joshua 15:5, and encoded across it are the words "he found the exact place, Lisan."

"Lisan, tongue of the Dead Sea, to the North," appears again in Joshua 18:19, an even more precise description of the location.

"Encoder" is encoded across the plain text that reveals the location. "Encoded" appears five times on the same table, and in Hebrew the same word means "hidden" and "North."

○ ENCODER ☐ LISAN, TONGUE OF THE DEAD SEA, TO THE NORTH

So the plain text of Joshua, the only book in the Bible that mentions Lisan by name, appeared to reveal the exact place on the peninsula to look—at its most northern point, where a finger of the peninsula went up into the Dead Sea, forming a small bay, a "tongue of the Dead Sea."

I looked in the Torah for "Lisan, tongue of sea," and it appeared just once with no skips. "The Lisan" was encoded across "tongue of sea," and "ancient key" was encoded across both.

I went to see Eli Rips. I showed him the encodings, and told him I had walked the ground.

מ ע נ י ש נ י ס ו
ע ש ר י ס א ל ק ו
מ א ת י ס ב ב נ י ג
ד ל מ ש פ ח ת מ ם ל
צ פ ו ו מ מ ש פ ח ת
ה פ צ ו ו י ל ה נ ג
י מ ש ע ה ה צ ה ג
ל ו ו צ ו י מ ש ע פ
ח ת ה ש נ ו י ל א
ז נ י מ ש פ ח ת ה
א ז ו נ י ע ר י מ
ש פ ה ח ת ה ע ר י ל
א ו ו ד מ ש פ ה ת
א ל י ו ד י ל א ר ר
א ל י מ ש פ ה ת ה
ש פ ח ת ב נ י ג ד ר
ל ק פ ד י ה ה ס א ר
ב ע י ס א ל פ ו ו ה ת
מ ש מ א ו ת ב נ י
מ ש מ א ו ת ב נ י

○  THE LISAN

◇  ANCIENT KEY/
   MAP OF SENSOR

□  LISAN, TONGUE
   OF SEA

□  ENCODED/NORTH

□  ENCODED/NORTH

Rips studied the code on his computer, and immediately saw something remarkable.

"The same letters in Hebrew that spell 'ancient key' also spell 'map of sensor,'" said Rips. "And that crosses 'tongue of sea' and 'the Lisan.'"

It was a crucial discovery. The only way I might find a buried "obelisk" would be with some "sensor," some advanced technology that could see underwater and underground and make a "map" of what was hidden to the naked eye.

The alternating letters in the two-skip code sequence that spelled "ancient key/map of sensor" made a new statement: "Uncovered, visible, discovery, detection."

Later, I discovered that this same remarkable verse of the Bible, in which "Lisan, tongue of sea" appeared with no skips in the hidden text, and "ancient key/map of sensor" was encoded across it, not only appeared with "the Lisan," but also with ten other central clues in my hunt for the "code key."

"Obelisk in Lisan" crossed "Lisan, tongue of sea." So did "map of hiding place." And "key" appeared three times on that table, where "map of sensor" crossed "map of hiding place."

Rips and I looked for "sensor marked the spot." Amazingly, it was encoded across the one place in the Torah where "the Lisan" appeared with no skips. The odds were 2 in 10,000.

And finally, sitting alone with my laptop one night, I looked in the most prophetic book of the Bible, Daniel, and saw that "sensor marking" was encoded there, too, with "Lisan."

O MAP OF HIDING PLACE    ◇ MAP OF SENSOR/ANCIENT KEY

□ LISAN, TONGUE OF SEA    ⬠ KEY    ⬠ KEY

O SENSOR MARKED THE SPOT    □ THE LISAN

The full hidden statement in Daniel was yet more extraordinary. It said, "Lisan as Siddim."

O  SENSOR MARKING            □  LISAN AS SIDDIM

It was absolute proof that I had indeed found the ancient Valley of Siddim. It was plainly stated in Daniel. The Valley was the Lisan Peninsula.

But the hidden message in Daniel was still more extraordinary. In the opening verses, the plain text tells the story of a siege on Jerusalem by a king of Babylon, who brought back to his palace some of the children of Israel. They were taught all that was known in the ancient world, "all wisdom, and knowledge, and science," including the language of the first known civilization, the "language of the Chaldeans."

Hidden in those verses was the entire story behind my quest.

In Hebrew, "language of the Chaldeans" also spells "Lisan as Siddim." Where the plain text of Daniel spoke of the children "standing in the palace," the same words in Hebrew could be translated "pillar in the palace." Perhaps it was the "obelisk" I was seeking, on which was engraved "all wisdom, and knowledge, and science."

But it was yet more extraordinary. Those same verses of Daniel told me the ✕ on the treasure map. "Mazra" also appeared in the same plain text that identified "Lisan as Siddim."

נ א ב ה ד ו ה י ה י ל מ ס פ י ק י י ו ה י ת י ו כ ל מ ל ש י ו ל ש ת נ ש ב
ה ל ו י י ס י י ר ב ז נ פ ש א ל ל ד מ ל מ ה ר מ א י י ו י י ל א ר צ
מ ה ס מ ה ל ה ו ן מ י ו [ס י ד ש ו כ ו ו ש ] י ר ה פ ס ס ד מ ל ל ו י ד ל מ ה
נ כ ח ל י ר צ א ש ט ל ב ל א י י נ ד ל ש ט י י ה ו מ ש ס י ט י ו ט
ר מ א י י ו ס י ס י י י ס ה ר ש י י נ פ ל ס י מ ה ר ל ו ז ס ⓗ ל ל א י
ד ל ע ט י ס י י ר ה ס ל י ש ו ג מ ר א ר כ מ ה ה א ל א ⓘ ו ר מ
ר ב ד ל ה ל ע מ ש י ו י ד י י ר ב ע ס ע נ ה ש ע נ ה א ר ת ר ⓦ א כ ו ד
א ה ס ה ל ו נ ת נ ס ה ע ב ר א ה ל א ה ס י י ד ל י ה ו ס י ◇⟡⟡◇
ה י ר ז ע ו ל א ש י מ ה י נ נ ל א י י נ ד ס ו ל כ מ א ⓩ נ א ל
מ ל ה ר נ ד כ ב ב ה ל ת ח י א ר ב נ ת ו ו כ מ ל ס ⓘ ת ש נ ב
ו ל ו ה ל ה ה ת א ת ע ד ל י ה י ו ר ס ע פ נ ת ו י ת מ ל ה ס ⓘ ל ח ד ל
ש פ ו א מ ל ח ו ה ו ו י מ ש ת י י ל ו נ ו כ י ת ב י ⓘ ו ד ב ע
י ד ל ב ל ק ל כ ו י י ב ו ז ו ת נ נ א ר ד י י ד ה נ א ר ד י י צ

○ SENSOR MARKING □ LISAN AS SIDDIM ◇ MAZRA

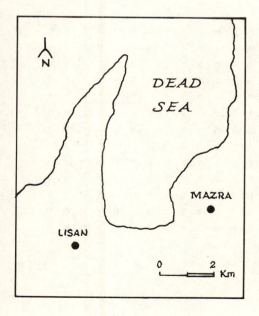

And "Mazra" was the name of the village at the southern shore of the inlet of the Dead Sea, the "tongue of sea" created by the "tongue of land" that jutted up at the northern tip of the Lisan Peninsula.

It was where I would find the "pillar in the palace," the "obelisk," the "code key." Every book of the Bible that I checked seemed to point to the same place—to the area that was once known as the Valley of Siddim, that was now the Dead Sea, specifically to the inlet at the northern point of the peninsula, the Bay of Mazra, and the finger of land that formed the bay, the Cape of Lisan.

In the Torah where "Lisan Peninsula" was encoded, "Mazra" crossed it against the highest odds.

O  LISAN PENINSULA     □  MAZRA

"Mazra" was encoded with "code key," and "obelisk" crossed both "Mazra" and "code key."

O  CODE KEY     □  OBELISKS     ◇  MAZRA     □  OBELISK

We had found the exact location. The only question was how we would now find the ancient object buried beneath it.

---

It would not be like it was in the movies. I would not be able, like Indiana Jones, to clear away some dirt with my bare hands and find the Lost Ark. Even with heavy earth-moving equipment, this X on the map, this pinpoint, was far too big to dig up.

I had no idea what the obelisk was made of, how deeply it was buried, whether it was under the land or under the sea, nor even if it still existed after unknown thousands of years.

There was one clue that Dr. Rips found, but it was not good news.

Where "obelisk" crossed "Bible code" the plain text stated, "The earth opened its mouth and swallowed it." If the obelisk had been swallowed, perhaps in the great earthquake that the Israeli geologist Neev told me shook that area more than 4000 years ago, then the obelisk might be very deep underground. It might have disappeared as completely as Sodom and Gomorrah.

It would take some very advanced technology to find it. What I needed now was the "map of a sensor." But when I checked with the experts, the geophysicists who looked underground for oil and precious metals and sometimes ancient artifacts, there was more bad news.

Ground-penetrating radar, which worked so well in finding objects buried beneath the sands of vast deserts, would be useless in the salt-saturated terrain of the Lisan and the Dead Sea. The radar would simply bounce back. It could not penetrate that ground.

I checked with my friends at Israeli intelligence, with the chief scientist at the Ministry of Defense, with people I knew at the Pentagon, and the CIA. They all told me the same thing. There was no secret technology that would penetrate that land, no new classified military technique, no advanced spy satellite that could find an obelisk buried beneath the saltiest place on Earth.

It was devastating. We had come so far. From a chance discovery of "obelisk" twice crossing "code key," against odds of a million to one, I was now perhaps standing on the very ground where the key had been hidden for thousands of years, led there almost miraculously, step by step, solely by a code in the Bible.

"I feel like I'm being led on a treasure hunt," I told Eli Rips.

"Of course," he said, assuming a divine plan, taking for granted what I could not believe.

"Why then has it been made so difficult that anyone more sane than me would have given up long ago?" I asked.

"In your question is the answer," said Rips.

He looked again at the original encoding of "code key." "This is really encouraging," he said, pointing to his computer screen. "It says, 'In our hands to solve.' It's even better in Hebrew—'In our hands to break,' as in breaking a code."

But the same Hebrew words also could be translated "in our hands for a crisis." And I was convinced that it was no accident we were seeking the code key at this moment of world crisis.

The background drumbeat of warfare in the Middle East gave the

O  IN THE LISAN PENINSULA          □  IN THE END OF DAYS

search an urgency that the Bible code only heightened. It warned that this quest was nothing less than a race against the countdown to the Apocalypse.

"In the Lisan Peninsula" was encoded with "in the End of Days."

The warning was clear, but so was the promise. Crossing "in the Lisan Peninsula," just below "in the End of Days," the plain text of the Bible stated, "For you and for your children after you, in order that you will prolong your days on Earth."

# CHAPTER THREE

# CLINTON

On television the President was confessing his sin, if not quite admitting his lie: "I did have a relationship with Miss Lewinsky that was not appropriate."

It was August 17, 1998. Bill Clinton was saying that he misled his wife and the American people. He was admitting in a solemn, grim-faced nationally televised speech that he had an intimate relationship in the White House with a 24-year-old female intern.

While Clinton spoke, I kept half an eye on the television, but I was focused instead on my computer, searching the Bible code.

Friends had been asking me for months to look in the code for the Monica Lewinsky scandal, and I'd refused to do it. It seemed too tawdry, too trivial.

But now it might cause the downfall of a President, the man who had brought Rabin and Arafat together, the one man who might be able to make peace in the Middle East, and prevent all the horrors the code predicted.

I knew "Clinton" was in the code because Bill Clinton was the first name I looked for in the Bible.

In June 1992, when I first heard about the Bible code, it passed my first test—it predicted Clinton's victory, six months before he was elected President.

"Clinton" was encoded with "President" in the 3000-year-old text.

○ CLINTON　□ PRESIDENT

In August 1998, as he confessed on national television, I again looked for "Clinton" in the Bible code, but now to see if it foretold his impeachment.

"Clinton" and "impeachment" were encoded together, very clearly, and against very high odds.

○ CLINTON　　□ IMPEACHMENT

And where "impeachment" was encoded with "Clinton," in the same verse of the Bible, the Monica Lewinsky scandal was also foretold:

"Hidden secret, lover of maidservant."

It was extraordinary. That's as close as the Old Testament gets to "young female intern."

○ CLINTON

◇ IMPEACHMENT

☐ HIDDEN SECRET, LOVER OF MAIDSERVANT

By the time I found that, the President had completed his five-minute confession, and the TV commentators were now saying that he might not survive the scandal.

While I searched the Bible code, I saw on TV over and over again the film clip of Clinton denying the affair, wagging his finger at the nation and saying, "I did not have sexual relations with that woman, Miss Lewinsky." And then again and again the instant replay of his just-completed confession, "I did have a relationship with Miss Lewinsky."

Until now it had seemed absurd to search for the outcome of this scandal in an ancient text that warned the world might soon face unprecedented danger.

But now, with the fate of the President in question, with the nation about to face its first impeachment trial in more than a hundred years, I did search for an answer in the Bible code.

When I looked more closely at the "Clinton" encoding I realized there was a second level.

The word right before "impeachment" was "against." The real message, the real match with "Clinton" in the Bible code was "people, nation against impeachment," or, more literally, "we will oppose impeachment."

And overlapping "people, nation against impeachment" the hidden text stated "their opinion prevented."

○ CLINTON   □   NATION AGAINST IMPEACHMENT

On August 17, 1998, on the night Clinton confessed, at the moment his presidency seemed most in danger, the Bible code predicted that Clinton would survive the scandal.

On February 12, 1999, the U.S. Senate acquitted President Clinton on both articles of impeachment after a harrowing year of scandal and investigation.

Once more the Bible code had been proven right.

---

Two years later, on October 16, 2000, I arrived at the White House to meet with President Clinton's Chief of Staff, John Podesta.

I was there to tell him that the Bible code warned that we were already in the End of Days.

The Secret Service agent at the gate was jittery. War had again erupted in the Middle East, and there was a terrorist alert. I had to wait half an hour to get cleared through.

While I waited outside the White House, I went over in my mind what I would tell the second most powerful man in the world, the man who sat in the West Wing and determined who the President saw, what the President saw, and therefore to a large extent what the President did.

Podesta had already given Clinton my book about the Bible code. He told me that the President had it with him at Camp David, along with a letter I'd sent him the day he announced a summit between Israeli Prime Minister Ehud Barak and the Palestinian leader Yasir Arafat.

My letter, dated July 5, 2000, stated:

"I've enclosed a copy of my book *The Bible Code*, because your announcement today of a Camp David summit meeting between Barak and Arafat confirms what the code foretold.

"The code, which appears to reveal our future, suggests you will play a central role in determining whether there will be peace or war in the Middle East, and that the stakes are even higher than you may imagine.

"I hesitate to state it in detail in this letter, because it sounds so Apocalyptic."

I could not bring myself to tell the President of the United States that we were already in the "End of Days." I could not tell him that, according to the Bible code, the world might come to an end within a few years. I could not believe it myself.

And I was sure if I did say it that the first person in the President's office who read my letter would assume I was one of those people who appeared every day in the park across the street from the White House, holding up crudely lettered signs that said "REPENT, THE END IS NIGH."

So instead, my letter continued, "In fact, I'm not at all religious, and I'm sure the disaster can be prevented."

The Bible code, I told the President, was science, not religion, and revealed modern names, places, and dates in a text that was 3000 years old.

"'Clinton' was perfectly encoded with 'President' against the highest odds," I wrote, recalling my discovery in 1992, months before he was elected. "Your election was my first concrete confirmation of the code's reality.

"Now I have discovered that crossing your name in the Bible is another statement—'he restored, repaired.' It has deeper meaning in Hebrew, 'to restore, repair, transform the world.'"

O CLINTON     □ PRESIDENT     ◇ HE RESTORED, REPAIRED

"The alternative is also starkly stated in the Bible code, the real Armageddon, a nuclear World War, starting in the Middle East. If the code is right, that danger is still years away.

"But what we do now, what you do now, may determine what finally happens. I think that's why the Bible code exists. To warn us in time to change the future.

"You may be in a far better position to end thousands of years of violence between Arabs and Jews than anyone inside the conflict," my letter to Clinton concluded.

"Camp David" was encoded in the Bible crossed by "city of refuge" in the plain text, and "peace" appeared in the same place.

○ CAMP DAVID    □ CITY OF REFUGE    ◇ PEACE

It was fitting that "Camp David"—the isolated retreat of Presidents, the site of the historic peace treaty between Egypt and Israel, and now the place that Clinton brought together two warriors, Barak and Arafat—was encoded where the plain text of the Bible laid out the rules that allowed murderers to find "redemption, deliverance."

But Camp David ended in failure. Both Clinton and Barak thought that they could make Arafat an offer he could not refuse. Almost everyone believed that within days, certainly weeks, Arafat would agree to accept a Palestinian state on 90 percent of the West Bank and Gaza, that he would surely accept most of East Jerusalem and half of the Old City. But Arafat barely even responded. No one understood why. No one understood the hold of religion.

Religion doomed the peace talks. The Bible code foretold it. "Temple Mount" was the predicted battleground.

Once the site of the ancient Jewish Temple built by Solomon, now the site of a gold-domed mosque, this 35-acre plateau in Jerusalem was the sacred spot no one would surrender. For Jews, the remnant of the Temple, the Western Wall at the bottom of Temple Mount, was the holiest shrine. For Muslims, the mosque on top of the mount they call Haram-Al-Sharif, was second only to Mecca. For thousands of years, Temple Mount had been the center of religious warfare, ground zero in the eternal battle for control of the Holy City, and it remained the one insurmountable issue at Camp David.

"Temple Mount" was encoded with all three names of the leaders gathered at the summit—"Clinton" and "Arafat" and "Barak"

"Temple Mount" appeared in the hidden text with no skips where "Clinton" was encoded, and the year of Camp David, "5760," the year 2000, appeared in the same place.

○ CLINTON ☐ TEMPLE MOUNT

"Temple Mount sabotaged" was encoded where "Arafat" appeared with no skips, again against very high odds. "Barak" crossed "Temple Mount" in the same place, and the original words of the Bible warned of the "End of Days."

**TEMPLE MOUNT SABOTAGED □ ARAFAT ◇ BARAK ◻ IN THE END OF DAYS**

It was extraordinary that all three players in the peace talks were encoded with the name of the holy site that blew the talks apart, and the Bible code seemed to suggest that an attack on Temple Mount might be imminent.

As the peace talks fell apart in July, as efforts to revive them failed in August, September, and October, I kept trying to break through, to reach Clinton, to reach Barak, to reach Arafat.

I arrived in Israel at the beginning of August 2000. The Camp David summit had just collapsed, and the Israeli government was on the verge of collapse. Prime Minister Barak was desperately fighting to hold on to his job, as his cabinet ministers quit one by one, and the Israeli people lost all hope that their struggle with the Palestinians would ever end.

Barak, now isolated and withdrawn, would not listen to the dire warning in the Bible code.

I had first tried to see Barak a year before he was elected. On May 17, 1998, when he didn't even know he would run for Prime Minister, I sent him a letter that stated:

"New information uncovered in the Bible code states that you may be Prime Minister at a time of very great danger to your entire country. I think that you will be the next leader of Israel, and hope we can meet."

The code even predicted the year, "5759," in the modern calendar 1999. It didn't seem possible, so I didn't include it in my letter—the next election was scheduled for the year 2000.

A year to the day later, on May 17, 1999, Ehud Barak won a surprise early election and became Prime Minister of Israel.

But I felt no sense of vindication. Only a terrible sense of foreboding. The encoding in the Bible that caused me to predict Barak's election a year in advance also warned of danger, and it was ominous and specific.

"Prime Minister E. Barak" appeared in a single code matrix followed by "crisis and death." The warning was explicit. The crisis would erupt at the holy place in Jerusalem claimed by both Muslims and Jews, "Temple Mount."

○ PRIME MINISTER E. BARAK        □ THEY WILL STRIKE TEMPLE MOUNT

Crossing "Prime Minister E. Barak" the hidden text stated, "They will strike Temple Mount."

So when Barak was elected, as predicted, when predicted, I immediately sent his closest advisors urgent messages asking them to warn Barak of the danger.

I sent a fax to the chief scientist at the Ministry of Defense, General Isaac Ben-Israel: "What worries me is that if the code was right in predicting his victory, it may also be right in predicting that Barak would be Israel's leader at a time of great danger."

But Barak, now so embattled that he would not see even the men in his own inner circle, said he was too busy to meet.

I sent the Prime Minister a new letter. It stated: "'They will strike Temple Mount' is just as clearly encoded with 'Prime Minister E. Barak' as the assassination was encoded with 'Yitzhak Rabin.'"

Barak knew that the Bible code kept coming true. The day Rabin was killed, Rabin's closest friend, the man who delivered my warning to Rabin, called Barak and said, "The American reporter, he knew it a year ago. I told the Prime Minister. It was in the Bible."

In fact, Barak had personally investigated the Bible code. General Ben-Israel told me that after the Rabin assassination the new Prime Minister, Shimon Peres, directed Barak, then a cabinet minister, to check it out.

"He also checked you out," said Ben-Israel. "He investigated whether you might be involved in the assassination."

I was shocked, but it made perfect sense. It was easier for Barak to believe that I knew a year ahead that Rabin would be killed because I was involved, than that a 3000-year-old code in the Bible had revealed the future.

"You were cleared," said Ben-Israel.

So Barak knew all about the Bible code. He knew that it had predicted Rabin's murder and his own election, both a year in advance. And yet he would not see me.

"Don't take it personally," said General Ben-Israel. "He won't talk to anyone now, not even his closest advisers, not even me. He's totally isolated now."

But I couldn't ignore the danger. "Temple Mount" not only crossed "Prime Minister Barak," but "Temple Mount sabotaged" was also encoded with "Ehud Barak" and "5760," the year 2000.

The danger seemed also to be encoded with a date—the "9th of Av." That was the day in legend that the First Temple was destroyed by the Babylonians in 586 B.C., and also the day the Second Temple was destroyed by the Romans in A.D. 70.

So on the morning of the 9th of Av, August 10, 2000, I went to see Barak's Cabinet Secretary, Isaac Herzog, the son of a former President of Israel, who had already received a letter from me and given it to the Prime Minister.

"Barak himself put security on alert," Herzog told me. "The Prime Minister is personally aware of the danger. There's nothing else we can do."

Herzog also told me that he had called the Jerusalem Chief of Police into his office the day before to alert him to the predicted attack, and that he had also warned all the other top security officials of the possible danger on the 9th of Av.

Everyone in Israel knew that an attack on Temple Mount could set off a Jihad, a holy war. Religious extremists of every stripe had tried to target it in the past, hoping to bring on the Apocalypse. The year 2000 was seen as the year of ultimate danger. In fact, an article in the *New York Times* asked: "In the coming year, the millennium year, during which some Christians are hoping that Christ will return—will someone attempt to destroy the Dome of the Rock or the nearby Al-Aksa Mosque in order to end the peace process or bring about the End of Days, or both?"

The leader of the Palestinian terrorist group Hamas, Sheik Ahmed Yassin, said, "This would be the end of Israel."

So I showed Barak's right-hand man Herzog that both "Barak" and "Arafat" appeared in the Bible code with the "End of Days."

"What does Dr. Rips think about this?" asked Herzog.

"He thinks it is absolutely beyond chance that 'Arafat' and 'Barak' would both be encoded in exactly the same place that both expressions of the 'End of Days' appear together," I said.

But nothing happened on the 9th of Av. There was no attack on Temple Mount. No religious fanatic, no terrorist, struck on that day. I feared that I had cried wolf, and that no one would now listen to me.

Still I asked Herzog again to arrange a meeting with the Prime Minister.

"Barak is seeing no one," he said. "It's impossible now."

So I turned my attention to Yasir Arafat.

---

On August 13, 2000, I met with Abu Ala, the leader of the Palestinian parliament, perhaps second in power only to Arafat himself. A short, bald, portly man who smoked a cigar, he looked like an Arab version of a Tammany Hall ward leader. But his office in the West Bank city of Ramallah was dominated by a big picture of the gold-domed mosque on Temple Mount in Jerusalem.

I gave Abu Ala a letter for Arafat. I told him it was a warning encoded in the Bible, a prophecy that Arafat must see. He read it carefully, and when he finished he was clearly shaken.

I'd expected him to be skeptical, even hostile. It was, after all, a code in Hebrew in the book of his enemy. But Abu Ala took it so seriously that he wondered aloud if he should send it to Arafat that day, although Arafat was on a state visit to China.

"We also have things like this in the Koran," he said. "Arafat is a good believer, so I think he will take this seriously. More than Rabin."

But months passed, and Abu Ala never delivered my letter. I couldn't reach Arafat. I couldn't reach Barak. So I tried again to reach Clinton.

In late September, with the peace talks hopelessly stalled, I sent the President's Chief of Staff Podesta a note:

"It's possible that the impasse between Barak and Arafat that won't yield to a rational political solution, will yield to a solution that meets the problem on its own terms.

"Religion is the problem. The Bible code may be the solution."

By the time I heard back from the White House, by the time Podesta agreed to see me, I was already back in Israel, and it was already too late.

On that day the new Intifada began.

Open warfare between the Israelis and the Palestinians broke out on Temple Mount, exactly as the Bible code had predicted. The day before I arrived, on September 28, the leader of Israel's right wing, the general who had vowed to crush Arafat, Ariel Sharon, led one thousand heavily armed riot police and soldiers onto Temple Mount. The next day, on September 29, 2000, after Friday prayers at the mosque, the new Palestinian uprising began, and four rock-throwing youths were killed by Israeli soldiers at Temple Mount.

The attack on Temple Mount finally came not from religious extremists or terrorists, but from one of the most central figures in Israeli politics, and it set off an endless spiral of violence.

"Sharon" was also encoded with "Temple Mount."

Every part of the Bible code prediction I had sent Prime Minister Barak more than two years earlier had now come true.

"They will strike Temple Mount"—the words that cross "Prime Minister E. Barak"—and the warning of "crisis and death," were all now a grim reality.

But still Barak would not see me. I went to see one of the few people the embattled Prime Minister still trusted, his brother-in-law Doron Cohen, a Tel Aviv

○ TEMPLE MOUNT   ☐ SHARON

lawyer. I handed him a new letter for Barak. But before he could read it, a call came from the Prime Minister's office.

"There will be no meeting now," said Cohen as he hung up the phone. "Two Israeli soldiers have just been lynched in Ramallah."

The images on Israeli television were horrifying. An angry mob had surrounded a Palestinian police station in the West Bank city, seized two young Israeli soldiers who had gotten lost and strayed into Palestinian territory, beat them to death, mutilated the bodies, and threw them out the window. One of the murderers held up his blood-covered hands, and the mob below cheered.

In retaliation, Israeli helicopter gunships leveled Palestinian Authority headquarters in Ramallah and Gaza. It was the worst violence since Arafat and Rabin shook hands on the White House lawn in 1993. It was war.

I had been in Gaza, in one of the Palestinian compounds that Israel bombed, just two days earlier, to meet with Arafat's foreign minister, Nabil Sha'ath. My driver left me off at the Israeli side of the border, and I walked a length of two football fields in the hot sun, across the no-man's-land to Gaza, on the twelfth day of the riots that had already claimed almost 100 lives.

U.N. Secretary General Kofi Annan arrived just before I did, and Russian Foreign Minister Sergei Ivanov was on his way, so my meeting with Sha'ath was delayed.

"What is this book with all this Hebrew?" Dr. Sha'ath asked me when I finally met with him, holding up a copy of my book about the Bible code.

I showed him the code table on the cover, where the words "assassin will assassinate" crossed "Yitzhak Rabin." I told him I had come to warn Arafat, through him, of yet greater danger.

"President Arafat believes in prophecy," said Sha'ath, no longer hostile. "This will affect him. In 1997 people who have ways to see the future warned him that his life was in danger, and Arafat was visibly shaken for months. His lip trembled. Everyone thought he was ill. But it wasn't that, it was the prophecy."

"I will give this to him but I have to find the right moment, perhaps when these troubles are over."

"By then it may be too late," I said. "I don't think these troubles will soon be over. If the code is right, the choice now is not between peace and street riots, but between peace and annihilation."

Sha'ath told me that he thought there would be peace. Two days later, the compound where we met was destroyed by a missile fired from an Israeli helicopter.

---

Now, two months after the failure of Camp David, with the peace that had once seemed certain shattered by open warfare, only two weeks after the President's Chief of Staff had agreed to see me, but in a world that had already changed, I stood at the White House gate, waiting to warn Clinton that we were already in the End of Days.

Finally, at 2:30 P.M. on October 16, 2000, the Secret Service cleared me, and I was brought in to see the President's Chief of Staff.

John Podesta, a quiet, rail-thin, reserved man, told me that he had personally given Clinton my book, and my letter, and would brief Clinton again about the Bible code as soon as he returned from yet another summit meeting with Barak and Arafat in Egypt, where the President was now desperately trying to arrange a cease-fire.

"I already have talked to the President about this," said his Chief of Staff, "and I will talk to him again."

"Any news from Egypt?" I asked him. Podesta just shook his head. "Nothing," he muttered. "Not good."

I decided to tell him the whole truth, because the danger looked so much more real now than it had just a few months ago when the Camp David summit was announced with so much hope.

I bluntly told Podesta that the Bible code appeared to state that we faced the time of ultimate danger long foreseen in all three Western religions, the End of Days.

I showed him the code table in my book where the two Biblical statements of the "End of Days" came together. And then I circled the names "Arafat" and "Barak" that appeared in exactly the same place.

○ END OF DAYS    □ IN THE END OF DAYS    ◇ ARAFAT    △ E. BARAK

Podesta studied it carefully. He looked at the names of the two leaders spelled out with no skips in a 3000-year-old text, each with a warning of the End Time.

"What does it mean?" he asked me.

"I don't know exactly what the 'End of Days' means, but it surely means a time of very great danger," I told him. "In the Book of Daniel, it says, 'There shall be a time of trouble, such as never was since there's been a nation.'"

"If we're talking about Israel, that's a large statement," said Podesta. But he knew quite well the Biblical meaning of the "End of Days." "What I want to know," he explained, "is what it means in the world today."

I showed him something extraordinary. Where "Arafat" appeared under "in the End of Days," the name of the Palestinian leader appeared as part of a phrase: "Arafat is being stubborn." "It got that right," said Podesta.

○ END OF DAYS    □ IN THE END OF DAYS    ◻ E. BARAK

◇ ARAFAT IS BEING STUBBORN

Then I showed him that where "Barak" crossed the other statement of the "End of Days," overlapping his name the hidden text stated "in a battle of your country."

○ END OF DAYS    □ IN THE END OF DAYS    ◇ ARAFAT IS BEING STUBBORN

◻ BARAK/IN A BATTLE OF YOUR COUNTRY

"Where's the good news?" asked Podesta.

I showed him that "peace" was encoded just above "End of Days." But then I also showed him that intertwined with "peace" was "terror."

O END OF DAYS     □ IN THE END OF DAYS     ◇ ARAFAT IS BEING STUBBORN

◠ BARAK/BATTLE OF YOUR COUNTRY     ▽ PEACE     o TERROR

"That's the good news?" asked Podesta.

"I think that's the reality," I said. "I think the best we can hope for is a battle between peace and terrorism. Even if peace is made, even if Clinton performs the miracle, the danger will probably not go away, and indeed will probably peak.

"There's an overriding statement of danger, very clearly meant for this moment, because it is mathematically impossible that 'Arafat' and 'Barak' and 'End of Days' would be encoded together by chance.

"According to the Bible code, this is the 'End of Days,'" I added.

"Now?" Podesta asked.

"If the code is right what's happening now is only the beginning. The ultimate danger is an 'atomic holocaust,' a possible 'World War' starting in the Middle East."

"When?" asked Podesta. "Where?"

"The code appears to state that World War III might start with an act of terrorism," I said. "'Jerusalem' is the only city named."

Finally, I told the Chief of Staff that the danger was clearly encoded with just one year—that both "World War" and "atomic holocaust" appeared with the same year, 2006.

"In five years?," asked Podesta.

"I know nothing about tomorrow," I told him. "But I'm certain the code is real, so I think it's likely the warnings in the code are also real."

Podesta seemed to take it all quite seriously. He said very little, but he listened intently, and took no calls while we met for almost an hour in the White House.

I told him I had just returned from the Middle East, and that what I saw on the ground made me worry. I told him I had already met with most of the people around Barak and Arafat, and that I saw only one real chance for a breakthrough.

"I met with Abu Ala in Ramallah, and I just met with Nabil Sha'ath in Gaza, and they both told me the same thing—that Arafat will take this seriously," I told Podesta. "Arafat believes in prophecy. I think that may be the opening."

Podesta seemed more focused on that than on anything else, perhaps because Arafat was, in the eyes of the White House, the problem. Clinton had spent more time courting him than any world leader, and was shocked when Arafat failed to make peace at Camp David.

I told Podesta that I thought perhaps the President was making a mistake trying to deal with Arafat as if he were Barak or Rabin or Peres.

"I think that Arafat is a mystic," I said. "He believes in his own destiny. He believes that he's serving some higher power. That's why I think that perhaps the warnings in the Bible code might reach him."

"Call me if you see Arafat," Podesta said.

At the end of the meeting, I asked Podesta if he was religious. "Yes," he replied. I asked him if he could believe the Bible code was real. "Yes, I can," said Podesta.

"Then this is probably a whole lot easier for you than it is for me," I told him.

Podesta laughed. "Clinton is also religious," he said. "I don't know if he believes in prophecy, but he is certainly religious, and he knows the Bible well."

"As a Southern politician, he'd have to," I remarked. Podesta laughed again. "He *is* religious," he repeated.

"Can you arrange for me to see the President?" I asked. Podesta told me he would.

"I'll let you know when," he said as I got up to leave. "I know it sounds ridiculous, given what you've told me, but it has to fit into the schedule. This isn't an easy time for him. He's only in office a few more months, and there's a lot to do."

As I walked back down the path from the White House to the iron gate, the enormity of the moment, of who I'd just met with, of what I'd just said, and of what was happening in the world right now, struck me full force.

Perhaps it was the setting—the White House, the undisputed seat of power in the world today—or perhaps it was the fact that I had just returned from two weeks of violence in Israel that shattered the peace that Arafat and Rabin had shook hands on at this very place seven years earlier. But there was something about the moment that felt very different than anything I had done before, and caused me to worry that all of this was very real.

Podesta, who had more access to the President than perhaps anyone, seemed to have accepted the reality of the Bible code before I arrived, and indicated that Clinton did, too.

The words I hardly dared to speak to him, for fear he would think I was crazy—"End of Days"—did not seem to surprise him at all, and he seemed to accept that as well.

That's when I realized that I was in a distinct minority. That nearly everyone else was religious, or at least believed in God. That people like the President and his Chief of Staff grew up reading about the "End of Days" in the Bible, hearing about the "End of Days" in church, and simply accepted it as real.

It was all quite strange to me. Here I was, in the White House, telling the President's top aide that this might be that long foreseen time of ultimate danger, and he appeared to be taking me quite seriously, and he said that he had already talked to the President, and would speak to him again.

So as I walked out of the White House, everything I had just told Podesta suddenly seemed more real to me—some terrible, even terminal, moment that was envisioned 3000 years ago, was perhaps now almost upon us.

# CHAPTER FOUR

# IT EXISTS

On the very day that the Camp David summit began, I found final proof that I was looking in exactly the right place for the "Code Key."

"It exists in Lisan" appeared parallel to "Bible code."

O  BIBLE CODE          □  IT EXISTS IN LISAN

But it was more than proof that I was looking in the right place. In Hebrew, the name of the peninsula "Lisan" also means "language." And the full code matrix that appeared parallel to "Bible code" therefore also stated "it exists in the language of man."

O BIBLE CODE □ IT EXISTS IN THE LANGUAGE OF MAN

"It exists in the language of man"—finally, proof that the Bible code was meant for us, meant to be solved by man.

I called Eli Rips. Everything I had found was the result of a new discovery by his computer programmer, Dr. Alex Rotenberg.

"Bible code" was encoded with a very short skip, much shorter than the odds would suggest. For Rips, it was an important new mathematical proof.

"It's a good, simple proof," said Rips, "because the same long expression—'Bible code'—appears twice with short skips. No one is likely to find anything like that in any text other than the Bible."

It had special meaning because "Bible code" was of course the most fundamental of all possible encodings.

But Dr. Rips was equally excited about my new finding. "It's a very beautiful find, no doubt about this," he said. "It means that the Bible code is written in our language, and that the code is therefore accessible to us, that it does not require superhuman knowledge or abilities."

The odds of "Bible code" appearing in the same place with the same short skip sequence as "it exists in Lisan/it exists in the language of man" were so far beyond chance as to be incalculable.

It was striking that this new confirmation of the "Bible code," and my search for the "code key," came at this critical moment for Israel, when the fate of the nation, and with it the fate of the world, might be decided when Barak and Arafat met with Clinton at Camp David.

Even as I tried to shift my focus from my archaeological adventure to the dangers encoded in the Bible—even as I tried to warn the President about the "End of Days"—the Bible code itself pulled me back into my quest for the "code key."

Perhaps it was now more important than ever to find the final proof of the code, so that its warnings could be fully understood, and would be heeded.

Perhaps this was the moment to unearth the ancient key that "exists in Lisan," that "exists in the language of man."

---

The new discovery that Rips and Rotenberg had made, and my sudden realization that "it exists in Lisan/it exists in the language of man" was encoded parallel to "Bible code," was the clearest statement I had yet seen that we were on the right course.

I reminded Rips that we had earlier found a very similar statement in the hidden text crossing "Code Key," in the same place that "obelisks" also appeared—"in our hands to solve."

It was almost as if the Encoder was openly encouraging the quest.

And there was much more on the new code table. In the plain text of the Bible, "two tablets of stone" crossed "it exists in Lisan/it exists in the language of man."

"Palace/Temple for the writing/writer" also crosses "it exists in Lisan." It suggested that we might find more than an obelisk, that the obelisks might be part of a palace or a temple, either built to house the code key, or perhaps the Encoder.

○ BIBLE CODE　　　□ IT EXISTS IN THE LANGUAGE OF MAN

⬠ TWO TABLETS OF STONE　　◇ PALACE/TEMPLE FOR THE WRITING/WRITER

Suddenly it occurred to me that the Encoder was revealing himself. The very fact that the code made a point of stating "it exists in the language of man," not only told us that we could read the code, but seemed also to suggest that it came from something other than a man, from some alien intelligence that wanted to communicate with us.

Also on the same table, the alternate Hebrew word for "obelisk"— "needle"—is encoded crossed by "he engraved, you will open."

This one extraordinary matrix seemed to confirm every basic element of my quest for the "code key." And it suggested that the quest would lead to something even beyond that.

There is a third way to read the same Hebrew letters that state the location ("it exists in Lisan") and that we can solve the code ("it exists in the language of man").

In Hebrew, the same words can also be translated "a man exists in Lisan." This seemed to suggest that we might find buried on that same peninsula that juts out into the Dead Sea, not only the origin of the Bible code, but also the origin of mankind, or at least modern man.

From the beginning of my quest, it had struck me as more than accidental that the very name of the place also meant "language," of course so appropriate to a code in the Bible. But also, more than that, "language" is so fundamental to mankind. It is the special ability that sets man apart from all other creatures on Earth.

And the second place-name, the name of the bay at the north of the peninsula, the location that gives us the ✕ on the treasure map, "Mazra," also has a significant meaning in Hebrew: "seeded." Together, "seeded" and "language" seem to reveal another, higher level of meaning.

So the third translation of the code matrix that runs parallel to "Bible code," "a man exists in Lisan," may point to the moment when modern man was "seeded," when he attained that special gift that set him apart, "language."

And there is a fourth way to read the same string of letters—"a man will return to Lisan." It was hard to believe, but it seemed to foretell our expedition.

Back in New York, I found a new code table that again confirmed Lisan as the location in a way that seemed beyond doubt, and again linked Lisan to the origin of language, to the location of the code key.

"Bible of Lisan," or "Torah of Lisan," which in Hebrew also means "the laws of language," or "linguistics," was encoded in the Bible crossed by "encoded."

Remarkably, the one verse of the Bible that names the exact place on the peninsula, "Lisan, tongue of sea," crosses "Torah of Lisan."

○ TORAH OF LISAN    □ ENCODED    ◇ ANCIENT KEY    □ LISAN, TONGUE OF SEA

And in that same verse, Numbers 26:15, "ancient key" is encoded across "Lisan, tongue of sea." In Hebrew, the same letters also spell "map of sensor."

"Encoded," which crosses "Torah of Lisan," appears twice in that verse, and in Hebrew also means both "hidden" and "north," again a precise description of the location, the cape at the northern tip of the peninsula that juts into the Dead Sea.

The double meanings of all the key phrases were too perfect to appear together by chance.

The very "laws of language" were encoded in the original Hebrew Bible, apparently the "Torah of Lisan," which would at once reveal the origins of language and be the "key" to the Bible code.

"Original language" was also encoded, and that in Hebrew meant "Lisan is the origin." "Code" appeared in the same place.

ת א ב ה נ ה ר מ א י ו ד ת ש א ה ש ה י א ו י ל א ו ר מ א י ו ל
ה ק ב ר ת ק נ י מ ה ר ב ד ת מ ת ו י ח א י נ ס מ ו ח ר ב ב ס י ה
ש י י נ ק ז ו ה ה א ת א ב ו י ד ל ל י ע מ ש ו ב ד ו ב ל ח ת ב ז
א ל י כ ו ד ת ה ל א ו ל ק ב ע ש ו י ו נ מ ר מ ש ה י ת נ ג ה
ב נ ו ק ר ר ו ` ו ה י י נ פ ל ה נ פ צ ה ב ז מ ת ה ד ר י ל ע ו ת א ט
א ת ש א ה א ב כ ש י ר ש א ש י א נ ה א נ ה ו ף א נ ה ת ה מ י י ת ו
י ת א ט ח ל ח ק ת ר פ ב ו ב י נ ר פ ו י נ מ ל ה ל ב ת ל ל ט ו
ה ר ש י ר א ת ב ם ו י ו י ל א י כ ל מ ה ת ת פ ש ו ל א י ד כ ל מ י ר
נ א כ ת ר ת ע ש ו ד י פ ל א ר ג ש ד ר ה ת צ י ו י ד ש ר י ה ת ו ד ג ד
ה נ ו ל ו ל ת ל א ה ת א ו י ד ו ל י א ו ה ה ת מ ה ט מ ד ר ה ה א ו ה

○ ORIGINAL LANGUAGE/LISAN IS THE ORIGIN        □ CODE

The proof that we were looking in exactly the right place for the key to the Bible code now seemed absolute. But more than that, it also now seemed clear that it would lead us to the origin of the gift that set man apart, language.

In some way, it was all about language. It could not be by chance that the name of the peninsula, "Lisan," in Hebrew also meant "language."

On my next trip to Israel, I showed Dr. Rips that "Bible code" was crossed in the hidden text by "dictionary," and that "Lisan" was encoded in the same place.

"Look at what the original words of the Torah state right here," said Rips, pointing to the very verse of the Bible, Genesis 10:5, in which both

◯ BIBLE CODE    ◇ DICTIONARY    ▢ LISAN

"Lisan" and "dictionary" were encoded crossing "Bible code."

"By these were the isles of the nations divided in their lands, everyone after his language," read the verse, which told of the origin of the first nations in the world.

In reverse, the same Hebrew letters stated, "You will search for the dictionary, something stolen, the gift of truth."

Then Rips saw something else extraordinary. Another verse of the Bible that dealt directly with language also crossed "Bible code," where it appeared with "Lisan," just below "dictionary."

It was the famous story of the Tower of Babel told in Genesis 11:7—"Come, let us go down, and there confound their language, so that they may not understand one another's speech."

The two verses of the Bible that deal most directly with language both crossed "Bible code" where it was crossed by "dictionary" and encoded with "Lisan," which also means "language." And on the same table, "key" appeared, crossed by "computer program."

I looked again at the encodings of "code key." And now I saw that "dictionary" also crossed "code key." Again, the extended statement in the hidden text was extraordinary: "The dictionary, and it was opened."

O CODE KEY          □ THE DICTIONARY, AND IT WAS OPENED

"Dictionary of the obelisks" was also encoded. "Tablet vitalized the obelisk" appeared in the same place. It suggested that what I was seeking was more than an engraved pillar, more than a dictionary in stone, but something that could be activated, perhaps some kind of computer.

O DICTIONARY OF THE OBELISKS     ◇ CODE     □ TABLET VITALIZED OBELISK

Finally, I discovered that both "Encoder" and "Decoder" are each crossed by "dictionary" in the Bible code.

○ ENCODER     ◇ DICTIONARY     ☐ HE WILL ENCODE

○ DECODER     ☐ DICTIONARY

All four of the most central expressions—"Bible code," "code key," "Encoder," and "Decoder"—were crossed by "dictionary." It could not be by chance.

It seemed clear that some kind of lexicon that defines the code, some "dictionary," exists in Lisan, the peninsula whose name means "language."

Would it be in Hebrew? Or in some other language? The code itself said only that "it exists in the language of man." Might it perhaps be the long-sought original language of all mankind?

Perhaps the "dictionary" might be like the Rosetta Stone, the tablet found at the mouth of the Nile 200 years ago, that allowed archaeologists to decipher ancient Egyptian hieroglyphics, the picture writing that appeared on the pyramids and the obelisks from the age of the pharaohs. That stone had parallel inscriptions in hieroglyphics and Greek, revealing the mysterious pictures as a language.

Might this "dictionary" in Lisan reveal a protolanguage of all mankind, "the language of man"?

I asked Rips if it might also suggest that the "code key" was in some language other than Hebrew, perhaps the original shared language of mankind.

"The original language of man is Hebrew," said Rips, with absolute certainty.

"Hebrew is the language of the Torah, and the Torah was created before the world," Rips patiently explained. "The dialogue of Adam with God is in Hebrew."

I suggested, gently, that the account of the conversations between Adam and God were in Hebrew because that was the language of the Torah, not necessarily because it was the language they spoke.

Again Rips was very definite. "No," he said, "the conversation definitely took place in Hebrew."

"But it's deeper than that," he continued. "The letters themselves, the roots of the words—they are not just symbols, but have their own independent meaning, and are each connected to the things they name."

Rips was invoking the wisdom of the Talmud and the Midrash, ancient commentaries on the Bible. All religious Jews believed that God created the Torah before He created the world, and that Hebrew was not only the original language, but that every word in Hebrew embodies the essence of the thing it names, and that each letter of the Hebrew alphabet was a building block of Creation.

"The language is part of the design of the world," said Rips. "The language preexists the world, because the Torah preexists the world. Since the code and the Torah were created simultaneously, the code also preexists the world."

Rips cited the ultimate authority, the sage who wrote the most famous commentary on the Torah, the Rashi, and showed me that where Genesis states "the whole Earth was of one language," the Rashi states "one language—the Holy Tongue (Hebrew)."

I admired Rips's certainty. But I would not be surprised to discover that the "code key" was in some language totally unknown to the modern world.

---

No one knows when or how language began.

So the Bible code's statement that "it exists in the language of man" was for me a puzzle, until a startling new scientific discovery was announced.

"A team of geneticists and linguists say they have found a gene that underlies speech and language," the *New York Times* reported in the midst of my search.

The new discovery, if indeed it proved true, raised an extraordinary question—when did this uniquely human gift come to be? Did it evolve? Or appear suddenly? How?

"The language gene" is encoded in the Bible crossed by a hidden text that appears to state the answer: "God's gene."

"God" gave us the gift of language, according to the code. It seems to have been a genetic upgrade. And the Bible clearly links "language" to the "code," as if the two were always intertwined, one inherent in the other.

O THE LANGUAGE GENE   □ GOD'S GENE

"Gene for language" is encoded with the words I first found with "code key"—"Mouth of the Obelisks" and "Lord of the Code."

O GENE FOR LANGUAGE    ◇ LORD OF CODE    □ MOUTH OF THE OBELISKS

"Language gene" was encoded a third time with "obelisks," "ancient key," and "Lisan, tongue of the sea."

○ LANGUAGE GENE    □ OBELISKS    □ LISAN, TONGUE OF SEA    ◇ ANCIENT KEY

There could be no doubt of the location. In Joshua, the only book of the
Bible that describes the exact site of our archaeological search, "language
gene" actually crosses the verse that sets the boundaries (Joshua 15:5)—"the
border to the northern edge from Lisan, the tongue of the sea."

○ LANGUAGE GENE    □ THE BORDER TO THE NORTHERN EDGE FROM LISAN

It is a perfect description of the cape at the northern end of the peninsula, where the Dead Sea becomes the Bay of Mazra. And on the same table,
the code stated the "language gene" could still be found there: "In perfect
condition until this very day."

But perhaps the most interesting encoding of "the language gene"
appeared in another book of the Bible, Ezekiel.

"Genius" crosses "language gene" and right below that, "in humans"
also crosses it.

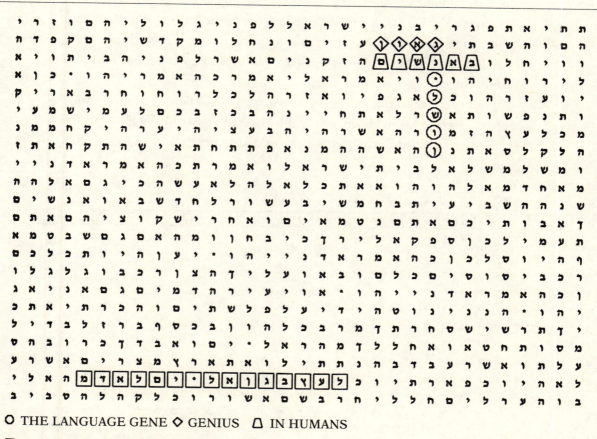

O  THE LANGUAGE GENE  ◇ GENIUS  △ IN HUMANS

□  TO DESIGN A GENE, GOD FOR MAN

And then, in the plain text of Ezekiel, on the same code table, the hidden words of the Bible state, "To design a gene, God for man."

The Bible code very clearly seems to state that man was intentionally endowed with a unique ability for language. It seems to confirm what the linguist Noam Chomsky first suggested more than forty years ago, that language is innate in man, that we have a specific neural circuitry embedded in our brains. It is the gift that makes humans human.

And in the code, this unique human ability to speak is linked again and again to the Bible code itself, as if to say that language and the code are one.

It is not only that "Lord of the Code" crosses "gene for language," or that time and again it is linked to the exact location of our search. It goes far deeper than that, again to the very essence of the Hebrew language, and the most ancient stories of our creation.

In Hebrew, "the language gene" also spells "Garden of Lisan." And where "Garden of Lisan" is encoded, the original words of the Bible state that "before the Lord destroyed Sodom and Gomorrah, it was like God's own garden."

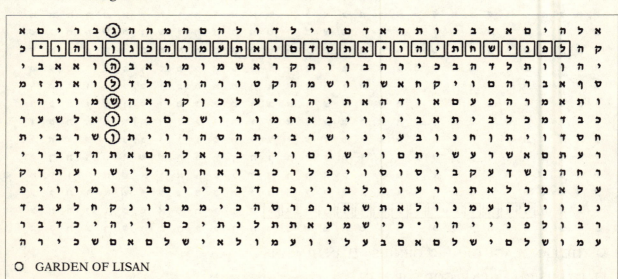

○  GARDEN OF LISAN

☐  BEFORE THE LORD DESTROYED SODOM AND GOMORRAH, IT WAS LIKE GOD'S OWN GARDEN

There is a consistent suggestion in the code that this now totally barren peninsula was once a veritable Eden, and perhaps that it was in some way linked to the origin of modern man.

Human speech was an intentional act of genetic engineering. That is clearly stated in the code. "I will place the language gene" is encoded in the Bible, crossed by "I will make intelligent."

O I WILL PLACE THE LANGUAGE GENE   □ I WILL MAKE INTELLIGENT

So the remarkable encoding, where "Bible code" appears with "it exists in Lisan," which goes on to state "it exists in the language of man," was more than a confirmation of the location, more than an assurance that it was meant for us, more than a promise that it could be solved by man.

It was also a statement of our unique genetic heritage, of that special moment when Man was raised above the rest of Creation.

"Birth pangs of language" is encoded once in the Bible, capturing the moment when man began to speak.

"Key," "obelisk," and "code" all appear in the same place, and again the hidden text states something magical—"his tablet vitalized the obelisk."

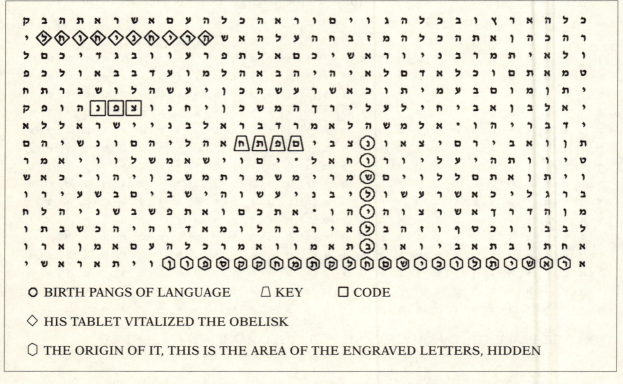

○ BIRTH PANGS OF LANGUAGE          △ KEY          □ CODE

◇ HIS TABLET VITALIZED THE OBELISK

⬡ THE ORIGIN OF IT, THIS IS THE AREA OF THE ENGRAVED LETTERS, HIDDEN

"Lisan" is encoded across "birth pangs of language," once more confirming the location, and its connection to "language."

It was another extraordinary code table that contained all the key elements of my archaeological quest. And the same words in Hebrew had at least three levels of meaning.

On the highest level it might be the story of the creation of language itself, in some long-forgotten time—"the birth pangs of language."

Perhaps this very spot, the northern tip of this peninsula, was in some way connected to the origin of language itself.

But the same words in Hebrew were also an idiom that meant "the difficulty of learning a new language." That again suggested that the "code key" might be in some language other than Hebrew, in some language no longer known to man.

Finally, on a very down-to-earth level, exactly the same Hebrew words had a third meaning, "the measuring lines of Lisan." It was a perfect statement of the method my archaeological team would use, the first step any surveyors would take: to lay out ropes to form a grid.

The hidden text crossing this one phrase that had so many meanings seemed to confirm all its levels: "His code, he will see its origin, because this is the area of the engraved letters."

I called Dr. Rips. Eli was almost as excited as I was. "Just technically, it is all quite remarkable," he said. "This is intentional, without question."

"Again, technically speaking, it's remarkable that 'code' and 'obelisk' and 'key' are all encoded in the same place, and that 'the Lisan' crosses 'birth pangs of language,' which also means 'Lisan.' It is definitely the code's way of confirming that this is all intentional."

I again told Rips that I felt like I was being led on a treasure hunt, given one clue after another.

"It's obvious," he said.

I told Eli I could not accept his conclusion, that there was never a moment when I believed it was more than an accident that I had stumbled across this, even though I did now accept that some intelligence does have the ability to communicate across time.

"Why can't you accept that this intelligence might have an interest in communicating with you?" he asked.

I told Rips, yet again, that although I believed there was a code in the Bible, I did not believe in God. And that even if I could believe in a God who created all things, including the code, I certainly could not believe that he would have any interest in communicating with me.

I said again that anytime it seemed like the code was speaking to me particularly, that "God" was speaking to me, it made me feel uncomfortable.

"You're not the first person for whom this is uncomfortable," said Rips. "Adam was also very uncomfortable with it."

———————————

There was something that made me more uncomfortable.

In Jordan, the Ministry of Tourism and Antiquities, which had already given me a written permit for the archeological expedition, suddenly refused to let our survey go forward. There was no explanation.

But at the same time, a local Jordanian newspaper published a front-page story, obviously leaked from the ministry, filled with anti-Jewish diatribes and total lies, claiming a conspiracy between Israel and my nonprofit foundation, Ark.

"What are the real facts about the relationship between the Ark Foundation's work and the Al Lisan area? Why would a Jewish foundation be allowed to dig for Jewish artifacts on Jordanian territory?"

I called the American Ambassador, William Burns. He told me we needed to take this false report seriously, because it reflected the true situation in Jordan. "You have to understand the culture," said Burns.

"This article has an ugly tone of religious and racial hatred, which I don't think Americans should ever tolerate," I told him.

"This is a powerful force in Jordan," said the Ambassador. "There is a blacklist against anyone who has contact with Jews here, and a very vocal movement against the peace treaty with Israel. Now is not the time to make any new contacts."

"No American official should ever excuse this kind of bigotry," I told Burns. "You can tell the Minister that I am sure it in no way reflects his attitude. But that if it does, I will confront it directly, both in Jordan and in Washington."

I knew that the new young King of Jordan, Abdullah II, had openly spoken out against the blacklist, had even arrested some of the opponents of the peace with Israel. But Burns cautioned against any immediate effort to contact the King.

"He's in a very difficult position," said the Ambassador. "Most of his population is Palestinian."

It was hard to wait. I realized how urgent my quest for the "code key" might be. The Bible code repeatedly warned that the key, the obelisk, might reveal some terrible horror yet to come, the ultimate danger we face, perhaps confirming what the Bible code had already revealed, but now in a way no one could ignore.

And by now, open warfare had erupted in the Holy Land.

# CHAPTER FIVE

# ARAFAT

At midnight on April 12, 2001, seven months into the new Intifada, an unmarked car came to my hotel at the border between East and West Jerusalem to pick up a letter I had written to Yasir Arafat.

"I have information that your life may be in danger," my letter to the Palestinian leader stated.

"The warning comes from the same source that predicted Yitzhak Rabin would be assassinated, a year before he was killed.

"The source is a code in the Bible that appears to tell the future—but may also warn us in advance of dangers we can prevent."

I did not expect Arafat to see me. I did not think the leader of the Palestinians would want to hear about a secret code in the Holy Book of his enemy, about warnings encoded in Hebrew in the Old Testament, especially at this moment of crisis.

Israel and the Palestinians were close to war. Ariel Sharon, the newly elected Prime Minister, had vowed to crush Arafat's uprising that had already left more than 450 dead.

But Arafat believed in prophecy. I had been trying for a year to reach him, and all of his closest advisers had told me that.

"Arafat will take this seriously," his foreign minister Nabil Sha'ath said when I saw him in Gaza at the beginning of the Intifada, just days before

Israeli helicopter gunships blasted the compound we met in. "He's a true believer."

Abu Ala, the leader of the Palestinian parliament, said the same thing when I met with him right after the collapse of the Camp David peace talks. But he seemed resigned, and assumed that Arafat's fate was sealed.

"So, it is the will of God," he said. But he agreed to deliver my letter to Arafat, and alerted the West Bank security chief.

But neither Sha'ath nor Abu Ala ever gave Arafat my letter. Both kept promising to do it, month after month, but never did. Finally, Sha'ath told me why.

"Arafat will believe you," he said. "It will scare him."

Now, finally, a year later, the letter had been delivered to Arafat—past midnight, as I was packing to leave Israel early the next morning.

And at 1:15 A.M. I was awakened by an urgent call asking me to come see Arafat the next day. "The President read your letter, he wants to see you," his nervous Chief of Staff said. "Will you please stay?"

I lay awake for the next hour. Arafat had obviously insisted on seeing me the moment he read my letter. In a few hours I would have to tell him, face to face, that he might be killed. Suddenly I wasn't sure I wanted the job.

I'm a reporter, not a prophet. But Arafat wasn't seeing me because I was a reporter, because I used to work for the *Washington Post* and *Wall Street Journal*. He had not granted an interview to an American reporter in at least ten years.

Arafat was seeing me because in his eyes I was a prophet.

I had enclosed with my letter to Arafat a very similar letter I sent his peace partner, the Israeli Prime Minister Yitzhak Rabin, a year before he was assassinated on November 4, 1995.

My September 1, 1994 letter to Rabin began:

"An Israeli mathematician has discovered a hidden code in the Bible that appears to reveal the details of events that took place thousands of years after the Bible was written.

"The reason I'm telling you about this is that the only time your full name—Yitzhak Rabin—is encoded in the Bible, the words 'assassin that will assassinate' cross your name."

Now, as I drove through the Israeli checkpoints to see Arafat in the West Bank city of Ramallah, along a road where motorists were sometimes ambushed by snipers, in a city where scores of Palestinians had been killed, and two Israeli soldiers lynched and mutilated by a mob at the local police station, I recalled the moment in September 1993 when Rabin and Arafat shook hands on the White House lawn, and peace seemed within reach.

Now Rabin was dead, as the Bible code had predicted, and if the code was right, Arafat also might soon be murdered.

At 9 P.M. on Friday, April 13, 2001, I arrived at Arafat's heavily guarded high-walled compound. I was hurried through the big iron gate, and led past groups of tense, heavily armed Palestinian guards, into a small meeting room. I had arrived half an hour early, but Arafat entered the room almost instantly. He knew why I had come to see him.

Arafat sat a foot away from me in his kefiyeh, the black and white checkered headdress he always wore, and his olive drab military uniform.

I again showed him the letter I wrote the slain Israeli Prime Minister Rabin, and the code table where "assassin will assassinate" crossed "Yitzhak Rabin."

○ YITZHAK RABIN   □ ASSASSIN WILL ASSASSINATE

"I mourn him every day," said Arafat, speaking to me directly in English. I could see a sadness in his eyes that seemed very real.

Then I showed Arafat the Bible code table where his name—"Yasir Arafat"—appeared with exactly the same words from the same verse of the Bible: "assassin will assassinate."

O  YASIR ARAFAT     □  ASSASSIN WILL ASSASSINATE

Arafat looked at it intently, and his lip trembled, and his hand shook, but he did not seem surprised.

I knew that he already believed his life was in danger, and had in fact used it as a negotiating ploy at Camp David. When President Clinton urged him to give up control of Jerusalem, Arafat asked Clinton, "Do you want to attend my funeral?"

Still, it is not an easy thing to tell any man that he might be killed, especially when he's seated a foot away. And the fact that Arafat so clearly believed me only made it more difficult.

"There are three clear warnings with your name," I told him, pointing to each on the code table, translating the Hebrew into English, while his chief peace negotiator, Saeb Erekat, translated the English into Arabic. Arafat looked right into my eyes as I spoke.

"'Assassin will assassinate,'" I said, reading the encoded words out loud, "and 'the ambusher will kill him,' which crosses 'shooters of Yasir Arafat.'"

○ SHOOTERS OF YASIR ARAFAT     □ ASSASSIN WILL ASSASSINATE
◇ THE AMBUSHER WILL KILL HIM

Erekat repeated it in Arabic. Arafat stared at me harder. His eyes bulged. "When will this happen?" he asked.

"I don't know," I said. "We can't find any date in the code, and I'm only a reporter. I don't know anything about tomorrow, except what's in the code."

Arafat looked deep into my eyes, as if to see whether I was holding something back. He seemed to expect something more from me, as if I myself knew the future.

"I don't even know if the danger is real," I told Arafat. "But I don't think the warning should be ignored. Rabin was killed when and where the Bible code predicted he would be, and the assassinations of Anwar Sadat and John F. Kennedy were also encoded in the Bible, in detail.

"So I'm telling you the same thing I told Rabin—I think you may be in danger, but I also think the danger can be prevented if the details of the warning are understood."

"If it is written, what can I do?" asked Arafat.

"I think that it's a warning, not a prediction," I told Arafat. "I don't think it's written in stone." But I knew I was going against a basic teaching of Islam, which said that a man's fate is sealed, his whole life is decided, even before he is born.

It was one of the reasons I had hesitated to contact Arafat. In fact, his foreign minister Sha'ath told me that Arafat had said many times, "God will determine what he wants to do with me." "He believes our destiny is ordained," Sha'ath had told me. "We do not have one day more, or one day less, to live."

But now I told Arafat that this computer code was different, that it existed so that we could change our future.

"The Bible code does not reveal only one future, but every possible future," I said. "What we do determines the final outcome."

Arafat smiled. He did not reply. I wondered if the smile indicated agreement, or just his conviction that he knew better and I had much to learn.

There was another reason I had hesitated to contact Arafat, and I stated it to him openly now: "I have friends in Israel, and even in America, who would never forgive me if they knew I had come here to try to save your life."

I am a Jew. And to many, probably most, Jews, Arafat remained a terrorist and a murderer. Indeed, Prime Minister Sharon had just called him that, in public. And on that very morning, when I told him I would meet with Arafat, the Israeli scientist who discovered the Bible code, Dr. Rips, had compared Arafat to Hitler and Saddam Hussein.

I didn't see him that way. I recognized that Arafat might be a terrible threat to Israel, but I also believed that his murder would end the last chance for peace. In any event, I felt obligated to warn him, to try to prevent another assassination.

"I'm here because I'm a reporter, and I have the same obligation to warn you that I had to warn Rabin," I told Arafat.

"Yes," he said. "A reporter can't take sides."

"Also, I believe your murder would be a catastrophe for Israel as well as for your own people," I said. "And I believe it's possible to prevent it."

I showed Arafat a second version of the same code table, in which the word "terrorist" overlapped by "Hamas" crossed his name—crossed "shooters of Yasir Arafat."

It seemed a clear warning that the extremist Palestinian group that opposed peace with Israel, and claimed responsibility for most of the terrorist bombings, might also try to murder their own leader, Arafat.

"Hamas," repeated Arafat, nodding his head yes.

○ SHOOTERS OF YASIR ARAFAT

◇ THE AMBUSHER WILL KILL HIM　　□ TERRORIST/HAMAS

I showed Arafat a third code table that Dr. Rips had found that morning. "They shot Arafat" crossed by "Ishmaelites," the Biblical name for Arabs, the sons of Ishmael.

| ל | ו | ע | ל | א | י | ו | ה | י | ש | ם | ב | ש | ם | ש | א | ק | ר | י | ו | ע | ב | ש | ר | א | ב | ב | ל | ש | א | ע | ט | י |
| ה | ד | ש | ה | ו | ש | ע | ד | ל | י | י | ו | נ | ב | ו | ש | ע | ל | א | ק | ח | צ | י | ר | ב | ד | ב | ת | ע | מ | ש | ה |
| מ | י | ר | י | ו | נ | א | ב | ק | ע | י | ח | ק | י | ו | ד | נ | י | ב | י | נ | י | ב | ד | ע | ל | ה | י | ה | ו |
| ח | א | י | ד | ו | ב | י | ה | ת | ל | א | י | ד | י | י | **ס** | **י** | **ל** | **א** | **ע** | **מ** | **ש** | **י** | ל | ו | י | ר | נ | ג | ל | מ | כ | ו |
| ו | ה | ל | א | ו | ש | ו | ג | י | ב | י | ת | ב | י | ש | **ח** | א | ם | ת | ד | ר | ו | י | ה | ה | א | ו | ב | כ | ל | ר | ת |
| י | ב | ס | י | ר | פ | א | ת | א | ס | ה | ה | י | נ | ש | ת | א | **ן** | ס | ו | י | ח | ק | י | י | ה | צ | ר | א | ו | י | פ | א |
| מ | א | ל | ס | מ | ה | ע | ל | א | ו | ר | מ | א | י | י | ו | **ן** | ט | ש | ו | ע | ה | י | ש | ג | נ | ו | א | צ | י | ו |
| ר | ח | א | ר | ש | ה | א | ח | פ | ה | ש | ר | ה | ל | ת | ב | ז | ד | **ע** | ו | א | ס | כ | ל | ל | ב | י | ש | ה | ה | ע | ר | פ |
| מ | ה | ת | א | ת | ב | ש | ו | נ | צ | ר | א | ל | א | ם | א | **ב** | ד | ע | ה | ג | נ | ש | ו | ס | י | ע | ר | ב | א | ן | מ | ס |
| י | י | ר | ב | ד | כ | ל | ת | א | ה | ש | מ | ב | ת | כ | י | **ו** | ה | י | ש | ע | נ | י | ו | ה | י | ר | ב | ד | ר | ש | א | ה |
| ה | א | ו | י | ל | א | י | ה | ר | א | ל | א | ה | י | י | ר | **ו** | ש | א | ש | ק | ה | י | ד | ג | ב | ל | ו | י | ה | נ | ת | ה |
| ה | ו | י | ת | י | ת | א | ו | ן | כ | ש | מ | ה | ת | ת | ד | ת | **ן** | ת | א | ר | צ | ה | ר | ע | י | ש | ד | ם | מ | ת | א | ה |
| ה | א | ו | ה | ש | מ | ו | ג | מ | מ | ו | צ | ח | ו | ר | ה | צ | ח | ר | ל | ס | ו | י | מ | ה | מ | ש | ו | ת | י | ו | ה | ב |
| א | א | י | ו | ה | י | ה | ו | צ | ר | ש | א | ם | י | מ | ל | ש | ה | ה | ח | ב | ז | ל | ו | י | ה | י | א | ו | ל | מ | ל | ו |
| ע | ת | ע | ר | צ | ר | א | מ | ר | כ | ו | ה | ת | ג | ב | ג | א | ו | י | א | ו | ת | ח | ת | ק | ר | ב | ת | מ | ד | ז | א | ה |

**O** THEY SHOT ARAFAT   **□** ISHMAELITES/ARABS

"Arabs, not Jews," I said.

Arafat looked at me, and at his negotiator, Erekat, and at his Chief of Staff, Abu Rudaineh, and nodded his head yes again. They all nodded in agreement. They all understood that if he was in danger, it was likely from his own people, that his killer would be an Arab, just as Rabin's killer was a Jew.

"Khomeini once put a price on my head for making peace with Rabin," Arafat interjected, referring to the Iranian ayatollah who ordered the U.S. embassy seized and the Americans taken hostage.

It worried me that Arafat might use my warning only as another reason not to make peace. He certainly knew that he was far more likely to be killed if he made peace than if he did not. Sadat had been killed by an Egyptian for making peace with Israel, and Rabin by an Israeli for making peace with Arafat.

"If you make peace," I told him, "you will be in danger. But if you don't, your entire people will be in danger."

It was really what I had come to tell Arafat. Not just that he might be killed, but something far beyond that. I had come to tell him what I had already told Clinton and Barak, what I was now trying to tell Sharon and Bush, the terrible warning in the Bible code that we might all be killed.

"According to the Bible code we are right now in an ultimate time of danger," I told Arafat. "Perhaps a time of danger greater than the world has ever faced, the time long foreseen by all three Western religions."

I opened my book to the page where both Biblical expressions of the "End of Days" were encoded together, and showed the matrix of Hebrew letters to Arafat.

"How do you say these words?" Arafat asked me. He didn't read Hebrew, and wanted to hear how the words sounded. He did not recognize the first, a phrase from the Book of Daniel. But when I said the words from the Torah, Arafat immediately recognized them.

"It's the same in Arabic," he exclaimed, surprised, once more speaking directly to me in English. "It's exactly the same."

"Judgment Day," said his Chief of Staff Rudaineh. "The End," said his negotiator Erekat. "The End of Days," said Arafat.

It was what I had most of all come to tell him, that we were right now in the End of Days, but I wondered if I had gone too far. I felt less like a reporter than an Old Testament prophet who had come to the court of a king to present a warning of doom from God.

I need not have worried. That was exactly how Arafat received the warning. I had reached him at his deepest level. "I already believed we are living in critical times," Arafat said. "Muhammad said that we have one thousand years, but not two thousand."

I understood his meaning—in the Muslim calendar this was the year

1422, four hundred plus years into the second millennium, the thousand years that Muhammad said we would not survive.

Then I showed Arafat what was not in my book, what I didn't know four years earlier when the book was published.

O END OF DAYS   □ IN THE END OF DAYS   ◇ ARAFAT

With a pen I circled the Hebrew letters that appeared just below "in the End of Days"—"A-R-A-F-A-T."

Arafat immediately recognized his own name. He had obviously seen it many times in Israeli newspaper headlines. He pointed to the page, and motioned Erekat and Rudaineh to come look. But at first he didn't seem surprised, or shaken.

Most men seeing their own name perfectly spelled in a hidden text of the Bible, in exactly the same place the Apocalypse, the end of the world, was foretold, would be shocked. Arafat seemed instead to have anticipated it.

Then I circled the letters that spelled "E. Barak," the former Israeli Prime Minister who had tried to make peace with Arafat at Camp David. His name crossed the second statement of the "End of Days." Then I circled

the letters that spelled the name of the new Israeli Prime Minister, "Sharon."
And then I circled the letters that spelled "Bush."

Arafat stared at the code table intently. Now he was shaken. His lip
trembled uncontrollably. His eyes bulged wider. He seemed far more shaken
by this than by the warning of his own assassination. Everyone in the room
was silent for a moment, taking in the enormity of the danger that was
encoded. And the extraordinary fact that Arafat, the leaders of Israel, and
the President of the United States, were all encoded together by name in the
same place, in the only place where the two Biblical statements of the "End
of Days" were also encoded.

Finally, Erekat broke the silence. "Where is the good news?" he asked.

I circled the letters in Hebrew that spelled "peace."

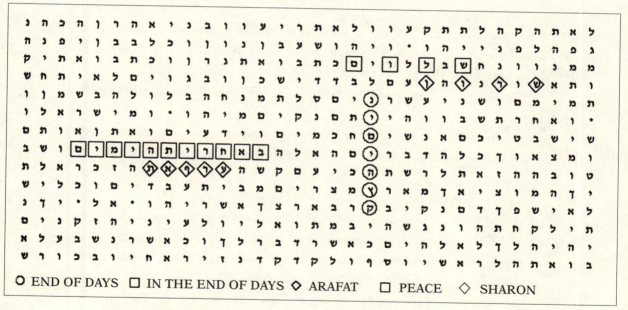

○ END OF DAYS   □ IN THE END OF DAYS   ◇ ARAFAT   □ PEACE   ◇ SHARON

"According to the Bible code," I told Arafat, whose eyes were now
locked on mine, "the choice is not peace or street riots, not even peace or
war, but peace or annihilation."

I showed Arafat two more code tables—"World War" and "Atomic Holocaust," both encoded with the same Hebrew year, "in 5766."

"That's 2006 in the modern calendar," I said. "According to the code, we have five years."

Again, there was silence. I told Arafat that I had checked every year in the next hundred years and only 2006 matched both "World War" and "Atomic Holocaust." I told him that the odds against that happening by chance were at least 100,000 to one. I told him that the odds against his name, and the names of the leaders of Israel and the United States, all appearing with the "End of Days" were a million to one.

But Arafat didn't seem to care about the numbers. I tried to tell him that this had all been computed by a very great scientist, the man who discovered the Bible code, but Arafat didn't care about science or computers. He heard me, he understood, but none of it mattered to him.

I had just presented the final proof, the indisputable hard mathematical evidence, and Arafat, who had seemed so totally convinced up until now, did not react at all. I asked him if he believed the Bible code was real, and if he believed that the dangers were real.

"Of course," he said without hesitation. "We have things like this in the Koran."

Arafat believed that what the Bible code predicted was real, not because it was found by computer, or confirmed by statistics, but because it was prophecy.

"If it is written, what can we do?" he asked me, again.

I told Arafat that it was like intercepting a comet that was about to hit the Earth. If we saw it coming five years ahead of time, we perhaps could change the trajectory, or shatter it, and survive. But if we saw it just a week ahead, it would not be possible. We would all die.

"A week ahead it would be as big and bright as the moon," said Arafat. "It would be too late."

"I think that the Bible code exists so that we will have an advance warning, enough time to save ourselves," I said. "But we can't wait five years and then suddenly try to do something. What we do today, what *you* do today will determine what happens five years from now."

Arafat nodded in agreement. "We have to act now," he said.

I then told Arafat what I had told Clinton in his last days in office. "I don't think there will be a peace treaty, or a lasting peace, until all sides understand that the only real choice is peace or annihilation," I said.

"The peace has to be strong enough to survive the next suicide bombing, the next shooting at a mosque or a synagogue, the next act of terror," I said. "The peace has to be strong enough to survive even the next assassination of an Israeli minister, or a Palestinian leader."

"Will you tell this to Sharon?" Arafat asked.

I told him I hoped to see the new Israeli Prime Minister, that I had already sent Sharon a letter, and that I had told him exactly the same thing—that according to the Bible code the only alternatives were peace or annihilation.

But I also told Arafat that the danger might not end if he made peace with Sharon. "I think the code states that some third party might attack with unconventional weapons, killing both Israelis and Palestinians," I said.

"Who?" asked Arafat.

"When you make peace with Sharon, I'll come back and tell you," I replied.

Arafat laughed. "You are welcome to come back at any time, as a friend," he said.

As I stood to go Arafat shook my hand, and then embraced me, kissing me on both cheeks. He took my hand again, and wouldn't let it go. No matter how many times I emphasized that I was only a reporter, that I knew nothing about the future beyond what was stated in the code, Arafat clearly had received me as a prophet, and still perceived me as one.

He held my hand all the way down the hall to the elevator, and then very sweetly waved goodbye as the elevator doors closed.

I knew his background. I knew there was blood on his hands. But I was sure that Arafat believed the warnings in the Bible code, and that he remained the best chance, perhaps the only chance, for peace.

CHAPTER SIX

---

# STEEL ARK

---

I saw two colossal pillars, perhaps the gateway to a temple or palace, perhaps the twin towers of some ancient city.

The vision vanished. I was left alone on the totally barren Lisan Peninsula, surrounded by the Dead Sea, trying to imagine the "obelisks" that once stood there.

But all around me I saw only the bright white lime that stretched for miles, the marl cliffs of the cape that revealed an ancient shoreline, and the thick crust of salt that the sea had left behind. I walked the ground of the surrounding reef, the lowest point on Earth, the bottom of the world, where the waters had receded, exposing land that had been hidden beneath the Dead Sea for 5000 years, since the dawn of human civilization.

And I wondered, even if "obelisks" once stood here, did they still exist? Or had they been shattered by time, and swallowed up by the sea? Were they only ghosts of a long-gone world, or could the "code key" still be found today?

I looked in the Bible for "key today." It was encoded in the verse of Genesis that also appeared with "Bible code" and "code on obelisk," the words in the Bible that first revealed to me the location—"the Valley of Siddim that is the Dead Sea."

"Key today" also appeared with the two locations that were named on modern maps—a village and bay called "Mazra," at the northern tip of the peninsula called "Lisan."

But even if I was looking in the right place, even if I was right now standing on the very ground where it was buried, even if it was right beneath my feet, I did not know how to find the "key."

The code itself said I needed a "sensor," some kind of advanced technology that could look underground. But no one could tell me what instrument to use unless I knew what the "key" was made of, from what stone, what mineral, the "obelisks" were hewn.

So I looked in the Book of Daniel, whose hidden text had already confirmed "Lisan as Siddim," and named "Mazra" as the ✕ on the treasure map, in a passage that also told of a "pillar in the palace," inscribed with "all the wisdom" of the ancient world.

"Key today" appeared in Daniel. But not with "marble," or with "granite," or with any other form of stone.

"Iron" crossed "key today." "A secret he did not guess, I will reveal" appeared in the hidden text overlapping "iron" where it crossed "key."

And encoded parallel to "key today" in Daniel, with the same skip code, was "Ark of Steel."

○ KEY TODAY    □ IRON    ◇ ARK OF STEEL

"It gives wisdom to the wise, and knowledge to those who have understanding," said the ancient prophet in words that crossed "key today" right above "iron."

"It reveals the deep and secret things," said Daniel, in words that in Hebrew could also mean "its container is deep, the hiding place." And that appeared right above "ark of steel."

The plain words of Daniel seemed to confirm the promise of the code key, and the hidden text did indeed reveal a secret I had not guessed—it was made out of "iron," or preserved in an "ark of steel."

I looked for "code key" in Daniel. "Steel" again was encoded in exactly the same place, crossed by "the Lisan." "Code" appeared twice more, crossed by "welded."

And again the plain words of Daniel seemed to confirm what the code promised: "Now I will tell you the truth."

○ CODE KEY   □ LISAN   □ LISAN   ▽ STEEL   ⬠ CODE/CODE   ◇ WELDED

I looked in the Torah, where I originally found "code key," twice crossed by "obelisks." Now I saw "steel" encoded there twice.

ו י ר ע ק י ו א ת א ש ת ו ה ר ה ת ו ה ל ד ת א נ ו ד י ו י ה י

כ ש ו ד ו א ת ה ז י ו ו א נ ת א ◇◇◇ ש ו א ת י ◇◇◇ ו א ו ת ב א ו ל ו

ב מ ק ו ם ש ר ד ר ב א ת ר ◯ י ע ב צ י ע ק ב ה צ ב ה מ ק ו ס א

ר ב ז ד ר ה נ ה ע ו י ס ר א ב ה מ ◯ י ו ש מ ה א ת ס א י ת ב א

ב ה י ח ת י ה נ ו ל נ פ י ה ב 〔ח י ר ו ת〕 ב י ו ד ל ב י ו נ ה י ו ס

נ ל ע ה ג ת נ ה ה ו י ו ו כ ר ב ◯ ק צ נ ר ו י י ת נ ו ג ת נ ת ה ל

ע ד א ת כ ל ד ת מ ב ה ע ל ה א ◯ ש י ר ה מ ה ס ד ל כ ה ל ה א ש

ל ע ה ז כ ה ס י ו ד י ל ה ק ה ◯ ע ל ע ל ע נ י ס י ה כ ת ל ת ה ל

ב א נ ו ד ת ו ש י ע מ ה ל ה מ ה ש ב ס ה י ק פ ה ה ע מ ו ש ד מ ו א ו

נ י י ר א ל ו ל ר ג ל ה ר ג ד ו ב ת כ ו ס ב ו ל כ ה ל ה ע ס ב ש ג ה

ס נ ו ה כ ס ל ה פ ל ס י א ל כ ו ב ס ל ו ל כ ל ש י ע ב מ ס פ ס ד

י ת א נ ל ה ל כ ה ה ו ל ה ת י ק י ה פ ו מ ש מ ה ו ס ט י ו ב ש ר ת ל מ ד

נ י ש ל ח ל ש נ ח ת א ה נ א ו ת א ה ב נ י ס ת ק ח ל ד ל ל י

○ CODE KEY     ☐ OBELISKS     ◇ STEEL     ◇ STEEL

It was hard to believe.

It was only 3000 years ago, at about the time that God gave Moses the Bible on Mount Sinai, that a new age of human civilization began—the Iron Age.

"Iron furnace," in fact, appears in the plain text of the Bible. Archaeologists have discovered iron implements from that era in Egypt and Asia Minor. But they have found only small objects, knives and jewelry, made by heating iron ore in crude pits, using charcoal.

Steel was also known in the ancient world. It is also mentioned in the Bible: "the chariots glitter with steel." But that appears in one of the later books, probably written nearly a thousand years after the time of Moses.

There is no evidence that a massive "steel ark" could have been forged before modern times, until the Industrial Age began in the eighteenth century. Archaeologists believe that a massive object made of "iron" or "steel" simply could not have existed thousands of years ago.

Yet "ark of steel" was also encoded in the Torah, and "Lisan" appeared in the same place.

The words in the plain text that overlapped "Lisan" were decisive: "this is the solution."

O ARK OF STEEL  ◇ LISAN  □ THIS IS THE SOLUTION

If the "code key"—the "obelisks"—were indeed in an "ark of steel," then it would be the solution.

An object made out of iron or steel would be possible to find. Perhaps nothing else could be found buried beneath the Lisan, the largest deposit of salt on Earth, the one place on the planet most difficult to penetrate with radar.

But anything made out of iron would be magnetic. A magnetometer would sense it, even deep underground. It would penetrate even the salt of the Lisan, even the waters of the Dead Sea. And nothing else made of iron or steel would exist in a place that had not been inhabited since Biblical times.

However, if we found a massive object thousands of years old made of steel, it would be an anachronism hard to explain. Even if it did not have engraved on it the key to the Bible code, even if it did not reveal a science more advanced than we have today, its very existence would raise questions not easy to answer.

Like the prophetic code itself, like the obelisks that legend said were made in Heaven, an ancient steel object would suggest an origin that was not of this world.

But if it existed, it could be found.

---

I went to see Eli Rips. I told him that the "code key" might be found in an "ark of steel."

To test that remarkable, but unbelievable discovery, Rips suggested we also look for "iron ark." It was encoded in the Torah. And then we both saw something extraordinary.

Exactly the same words that appeared with "steel ark" crossed "iron ark"—the name of the peninsula, "Lisan," overlapped by "this is the solution."

○ IRON ARK   ◇ LISAN   ☐ THIS IS THE SOLUTION   ◇ MAZRA

"Mazra" appeared right above "Lisan." There could be no doubt that the Bible code clearly stated that some "iron" or "steel" container existed in exactly the place I was searching for the code key, the obelisks.

Rips had been skeptical. But now he had to admit that the same unique phrase from the Bible, the same place-names, appearing with "iron ark" just as they had appeared with "steel ark," was nothing short of amazing.

"There's a mathematical term for this," said Rips. "It's called 'recombination.' You take a certain vocabulary, and recombine it in all possible combinations, and you find an unusual degree of correlation between the words. It's a good experiment."

"It is remarkable," said Rips. "I cannot deny it is intentional—of course it is—but how to explain it? What does it mean? I don't know. I can only observe the consistency, and I can only say that mathematically it is far beyond chance."

"Why would the code so consistently, so intentionally, lead me to this place, put an ✕ on the treasure map, if there were no treasure?" I asked. Rips, as always, would not even guess.

"I cannot say whether what we find in the code reflects or foretells what we will find in the real world," he said. "But the consistency of the encoding is just as interesting, and just as significant, if we find the obelisk or we don't."

Perhaps for a mathematician. Perhaps for a religious man. But I wanted physical proof. And now I felt a step closer to getting it.

"This is the solution." I felt certain that it could not be by chance that these words overlapped "Lisan" exactly where both "steel ark" and "iron ark" were encoded.

---

"Ark." In Hebrew, as in English, an ark is merely a chest, perhaps holding something holy, but still just a box. But the best known ark, of course, is Noah's Ark. And it was a vehicle.

I looked in the Bible code for "steel vehicle." It appeared, crossed by words in the plain text that said, "his vehicle He threw into the sea."

O STEEL, VEHICLE    □ HIS VEHICLE HE THREW INTO THE SEA    ◇ STEEL/STEEL

Those words came from the famous verse of Exodus that tells how God saved the ancient Israelites by parting the waters of the Red Sea, and then drowning the Egyptians who pursued them.

I wondered if it might also reveal some ancient vehicle now lost beneath the Dead Sea, the "steel ark" I was seeking.

"Steel" appeared twice more, overlapping "pillar" and crossing "steel vehicle."

"Iron vehicle" was also encoded, and again the original words of the Bible that crossed it seemed to tell two different stories.

The traditional translation of the plain text told of the building of the tabernacle, the portable temple that the ancient Israelites used during their exodus from Egypt.

"He has filled him with the spirit of God, and wisdom, and understanding, and knowledge," states the verse of Exodus about the artisan who built the tabernacle, "to make all manner of artistic work."

But where those words crossed "iron vehicle," the same Hebrew letters also spelled "forged iron, all the work of the computer."

"Lisan" appears in the hidden text just above "iron vehicle," and "cape, welded" crosses "iron."

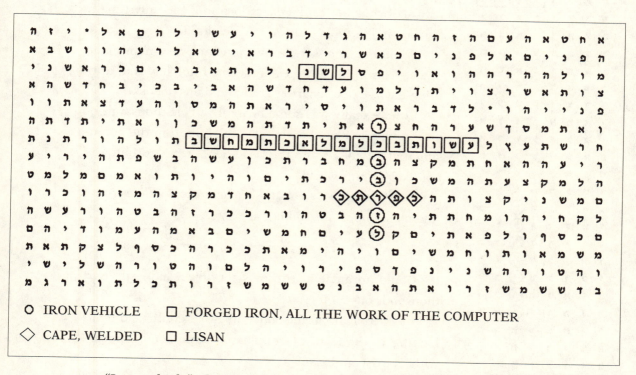

O IRON VEHICLE    □ FORGED IRON, ALL THE WORK OF THE COMPUTER
◇ CAPE, WELDED    □ LISAN

"Iron vehicle" also appears twice in the original text of the Book of Joshua. Once more, the ancient words appear to have two very different meanings.

"All the Canaanites that dwell in the land of the valley have chariots of iron," reads the traditional translation, warning of the great power of the people dwelling in the Promised Land.

Joshua, the leader of the Israelites, assures them "thou shalt drive out the Canaanites, though they have iron chariots."

But both times "iron vehicle" appears in Joshua, it is encoded with "tel of the obelisks."

A "tel" is an archaeological site, a mound of earth covering the remnant of ancient ruins.

"He found the exact place, Lisan" is also encoded with "iron vehicle." And that appears exactly where the plain text of Joshua states the exact location, the only time it appears in the Bible: "Lisan, tongue of sea."

Could the iron vehicle I was seeking be a man-made object from Biblical times? It seemed unlikely that anything the size of a "chariot" could hold an "obelisk."

If there really was some form of vehicle thousands of years old, made out of iron or steel, buried in the peninsula that jutted out into the Dead Sea, then its origin was not likely of this world.

What was this "steel ark"? Where did it come from? And most important, did it still exist?

---

Could an ancient iron or steel object have survived thousands of years?

I looked again at the code table that confirmed I was looking in the right place, where "Bible code" appears with "it exists in Lisan."

Now I saw that the hidden text crossing "Bible code" also stated "in a vehicle there, until this day."

"Steel" was encoded in the same verse of the Bible. And, if the code was right, the "vehicle" still lay buried on the tongue-shaped peninsula.

But when I returned to the Lisan with a Jordanian archaeologist from the Department of Antiquities, he

○ TEL OF THE
　 OBELISKS

□ IRON VEHICLE

□ IRON VEHICLE

○ BIBLE CODE  □ IT EXISTS IN LISAN  ◇ IN A VEHICLE THERE, UNTIL THIS DAY

questioned whether any iron object could still exist, especially in that salt-soaked ground, or the surrounding Dead Sea.

The top Israeli geophysicist I consulted, an expert in detecting iron underground, said that even if some remnant of the object had survived, if it was rusted it could not be seen by a magnetometer.

Suddenly, my entire quest was thrown into doubt. It seemed obvious that if the "steel ark" was underwater, it would rust. If it was in salt water, it would rust even faster. Even if it was buried underground, in this damp salty land it would surely have disintegrated long ago.

And the Lisan Peninsula was the highest concentration of salt in the world, a rock salt dome miles deep, surrounded by a sea so salty that nothing could live in it, which was why it was called the Dead Sea.

I called every expert I could find. One after another told me that any iron object would surely have been reduced to rust and dust millennia ago.

Archaeologists, metallurgists, and museum curators all said that almost all ancient iron objects that had ever been found were completely corroded, and that the corrosion would be sharply accelerated by salt. Most iron objects disappear in just a few years. None would survive for centuries.

I was devastated. I feared my quest had come to an abrupt end. But I could not give up. I made one more call.

Ronald Latanision is MIT's top expert on corrosion, on the survival of iron and steel. I asked him whether any iron object might survive for thousands of years underwater.

"It depends on how high the concentration of salt is," said Latanision.

I didn't want to tell him it was the Dead Sea, the highest concentration of salt on Earth, but I had to.

"Then it might still exist," said Latanision.

In the unique environment of the Lisan, of the Dead Sea, all the rules were reversed. It was the single exception to everything everyone else had told me.

"It's true that water rusts, and that salt accelerates corrosion," said Latanision, "but if the concentration of salt is very high, it can actually prevent corrosion. When you reach 35 percent salt in water, the oxygen drops very quickly. Without oxygen, there is no rust."

I called David Neev in Israel. I asked the geologist, who is the top expert on the Dead Sea, if the concentration of salt there was above or below 35 percent.

"Above," said Neev. "It's unique, the only place in the world."

Neev confirmed to me what the MIT expert had said. An iron object sunk deep in the Dead Sea would almost certainly have survived, because the water is totally devoid of oxygen. And without oxygen, there is no rust.

What if the "steel ark" was buried in the ground, I asked Neev and Latanision.

An iron object buried in the mud or clay of the Lisan would probably also survive, because the ground there is almost impenetrable to air, said Neev. An iron object buried in the rock salt that underlies the entire Lisan peninsula could survive indefinitely, said Latanision.

"A salt cavern would absorb moisture," said the MIT professor. "Without moisture, there is no rust. Without oxygen, there is no rust. Any airtight or watertight cave, cellar, or capsule would preserve an iron or steel object."

I was looking in the one place on Earth where a "steel ark" could have survived for thousands of years.

I looked in the Bible code for final confirmation. "Steel did not rust" was encoded once in the Bible. "Preserved," and "detection, revelation" appeared in the same place.

○ STEEL DID NOT RUST  □ IT WAS PRESERVED  ◇ DETECTION, REVELATION

The code key might still exist, preserved in steel. But there was a consistent suggestion in the Bible code that I might not need to mount an expedition, to send in a team of geophysicists with a magnetometer, in order to find the obelisks.

"Saved in steel" was also encoded with the location, "across the sea on the border of Moab," the Biblical name for Jordan. And right there, the hidden text stated "you will see it from there, a tiny tip of it."

O  SAVED IN STEEL    □  ACROSS THE SEA, ON THE BORDER OF MOAB (JORDAN)
◇  YOU WILL SEE IT FROM THERE, A TINY TIP OF IT

It suggested that the code key might be found easily, even accidentally, that the obelisk might just poke out of the ground.

"Obelisk sticking out, obvious" was also encoded, with both "Mazra" and "Lisan."

"From Lisan, it stuck out" appeared with the same words from the plain text of the Bible that crossed "steel ark" and "iron ark"—"this is the solution," overlapped by "Lisan."

○ FROM LISAN, IT STUCK OUT   ◇ LISAN   □ THIS IS THE SOLUTION

And the unique geography of the peninsula made it all plausible. I was looking for the code key on land that had been underwater for 5000 years. The Dead Sea was now at its lowest level since the dawn of human civilization, and it was still sinking rapidly. And the newly exposed land itself was sinking at a very fast rate. Indeed, an Israeli geologist had just published a report, "The Lowest Place on Earth Is Subsiding."

It was just barely possible that an object buried for thousands of years might suddenly emerge, on its own.

There was just one problem. An iron or steel object that had been preserved underground or undersea for thousands of years would disintegrate the minute it was unearthed or pulled out of the water. As soon as it was exposed to the air, to oxygen, what had survived for millennia would disappear in days, even hours.

Suddenly, my quest had become more urgent.

---

On October 5, 2000, I flew to Amman, Jordan, to see the American Ambassador, William Burns. He had promised to contact top Jordanian officials, even the new king, Abdullah II, to push them to allow our archaeological survey to go forward without delay.

But when I arrived, the American Embassy was surrounded by 20,000 angry demonstrators, shouting anti-Israeli and anti-American slogans.

Across the border in Israel, nearly 100 Palestinians had already been killed in the new Intifada that erupted at Temple Mount in Jerusalem a week earlier. Israeli tanks and helicopters were attacking the West Bank and Gaza. Many of the demonstrators outside the Embassy held up pictures of a twelve-year-old Palestinian boy who had been shot by Israeli soldiers.

The riots spread through the refugee camps outside Amman, into the universities, and now were threatening to bring down the Jordanian government.

Inside the American Embassy, Ambassador Burns was clearly shaken. He told me it would be very difficult to persuade the Jordanians to let me do an archaeological survey in the Lisan, just across the Dead Sea from Israel.

"Now is not the time to even ask," he said.

Three days later I did meet with the Minister of Tourism and Antiquities, and with the Deputy Prime Minister of Jordan, and they assured me that the expedition could go forward. But not now.

The new warfare in Israel suddenly threatened to prevent us from finding the "code key," just at the moment when the Bible code's warnings started to come true, when the entire Middle East seemed about to explode, setting off World War III.

# CHAPTER SEVEN

# SHARON

"I'm doing better with the Arabs than the Jews," I told the Prime Minister's son, Omri Sharon.

Omri laughed. I had just met with Yasir Arafat, who accepted without question a hidden code in the Hebrew Bible, but I could not arrange a meeting with Omri's father, the new Israeli Prime Minister, Ariel Sharon.

It was Tuesday, April 17, 2001. The night before Israeli tanks had invaded Gaza, entering Palestinian territory for the first time since the Oslo peace accords in 1993. So I was surprised that Omri met with me in the midst of this crisis.

I immediately recognized him. His face had just been on the front page of every Israeli newspaper, when it was revealed that the Prime Minister had been using his 36-year-old son as a secret emissary to Arafat. The left was enraged because Sharon was bypassing his Foreign Minister, Shimon Peres. The right was enraged because Sharon had promised he would not negotiate at all under fire.

But Omri was his father's closest confidant, his most trusted adviser. Some said that he was the second most powerful man in Israel. He was certainly the most savvy backroom operator.

We sat together on the patio of the King David Hotel overlooking the

Old City, the stone-walled Biblical Jerusalem, that was now the primary battleground of the Israeli-Palestinian conflict.

The new Intifada was into its seventh month, nearly 500 were already
dead, and now, by sending tanks into Gaza, Sharon seemed ready to declare
all-out war.

Indeed, it was Sharon who many blamed for setting off the uprising by
visiting Temple Mount—the one site in Israel most holy to Arabs and Jews—
with 1000 heavily armed soldiers and riot police in the aftermath of the
failed Camp David peace talks.

And now, the right-wing general who triggered the bloodshed was the
new Prime Minister of Israel. No one, including Sharon himself, thought it
was possible.

But it had all been foreseen in the Bible code.

"When no one thought your father would even be a candidate, the code
predicted he would be Prime Minister," I told Omri, handing him the code
table that foresaw the February 6, 2001, election.

"'Sharon' was encoded with the Hebrew date, '13 Shevat,' and 'Prime
Minister Sharon' was encoded with the Hebrew year, 'in 5761.' That's February 6, 2001."

O  13 SHEVAT/FEBRUARY 6, 2001    □ SHARON

Omri examined the code table skeptically. "I don't believe in this kind of thing," he said. "You can find anything you want to."

"But we found it two months in advance," I told Omri. "It keeps coming true. The Bible code accurately forecast the outcome of the last three Israeli elections—and not one poll got any of them right."

Omri was not moved. "If I can't bite it, I don't believe it," he said. "My father is the same way."

Ariel Sharon is not merely down-to-earth, he's a truly earthy man. He grew up on a farm. He's defiantly secular. There is not a hint of the mystical in him. He is not an intellectual, like Peres. He is not fascinated by abstract concepts, like Barak. And he is certainly not a true believer, like Arafat.

Most of the world does not realize it, but Israel is not a theocracy. At least half the country is totally secular, and there has never been a religious Prime Minister.

If Sharon has a religion, it is the defense of the Land of Israel by any means necessary. He believes that the Arabs hate the Jews, and that will never change. Before Sharon thought he could ever be Prime Minister, when no one gave him a chance, he made his position on peace very clear: "You know my position about it. It cannot be achieved."

"The Arabs don't want the Jews to be here," he said in that preelection interview. "That is the secret of this whole story. They want to take this land by violence."

"I will defend the lives of Israeli citizens," Sharon said. "And I don't think I have to elaborate. The Arabs know me. And I know them."

That is Sharon's religion.

I knew that it would not be easy to sell the Bible code to Ariel Sharon. But I also knew that Omri was the best back channel to the Prime Minister, that he had argued against his father's visit to Temple Mount, that he spoke to Arab leaders of his own generation, that he wanted peace.

I gave Omri a copy of the letter I had sent Yitzhak Rabin a year before the Prime Minister was assassinated.

"Show me this," he said, pointing to the place in my letter where I told

Rabin, "The only time your full name—Yitzhak Rabin—is encoded in the Bible, the words 'assassin that will assassinate' cross your name."

I handed Omri a copy of my book with that Bible code table on the cover. "And you sent Rabin this letter in 1994?" he asked. "A year before he was killed?"

It was the first time Omri seemed engaged.

"Yes," I told him. "The code not only predicted Rabin would be killed, but stated the year he would die, and we later found the name of his assassin in the same place. Rabin read the letter, but he ignored the warning."

Omri was silent for a moment. He studied the code table.

"So why did you want to see me?" he asked.

I showed him the same code table I had shown Arafat, where both statements of the "End of Days" appeared together, and "Arafat" and "Bush" appeared with "Sharon."

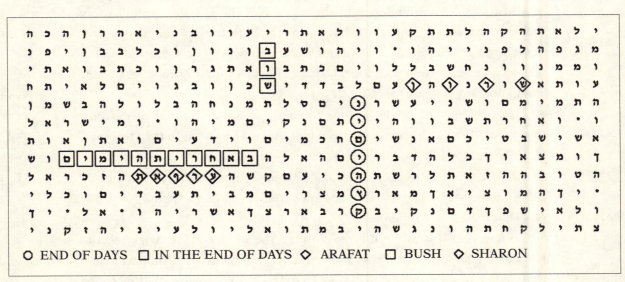

○ END OF DAYS   ☐ IN THE END OF DAYS   ◇ ARAFAT   ☐ BUSH   ◇ SHARON

"The odds against that happening by chance are at least a million to one," I said.

"It's just statistics," said Omri. "You can do anything with statistics."

"Even if you can't believe there's a code in the Bible that reveals the future, even if your father can't, it may still be important that I see him, because Arafat believes in it totally," I told Omri.

Omri knew that I had seen Arafat just days after he met secretly with the Palestinian leader. "At the risk of offending you," I said, "I think Arafat took the Bible code more seriously than anything you told him, because he believes in prophecy. This reaches him where he lives."

"I know how to talk to Arabs," said Omri.

"He's not a Westerner," I said.

"I'm not either," said Omri. "I'm from the Middle East, and I understand how Arafat thinks."

"I don't think Barak or Clinton did," I commented.

"You're right," said Omri.

I handed Omri a letter I had written to the Prime Minister and said, "Your father might be more open to this because he has a strong sense of his own destiny."

"I wish he was less that way," said Omri. "His life would be a lot easier."

He again read my letter slowly and carefully, and then asked a question: "I see only dangers. Where is the solution?"

"The Bible code only gives us information," I told him. "It doesn't tell us what to do. But it seems to say that your father can make peace."

I showed him that where "Sharon" was encoded with the "End of Days," "peace" was also encoded.

And I showed him that where "atomic holocaust" appeared, "Sharon" was again encoded with "treaty of peace."

Omri reread a few paragraphs of my letter, and when he finished he said he would give the letter to his father that same day.

My letter to Sharon stated:

"I've asked your son Omri to give you this letter and arrange for us to meet, because the code warns that Israel may face terrible, even terminal danger.

"This critical moment in Israel's history was without doubt clearly foreseen.

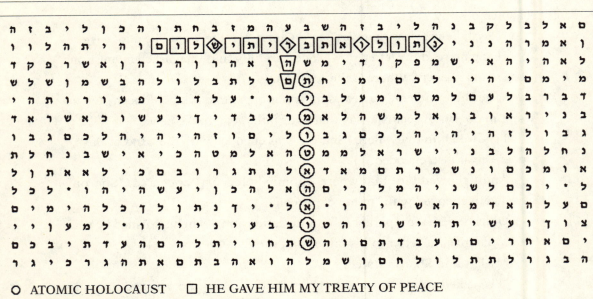

○ END OF DAYS    □ IN THE END OF DAYS    ◇ ARAFAT    ☐ BUSH    ◇ SHARON

⌂ PEACE

○ ATOMIC HOLOCAUST    □ HE GAVE HIM MY TREATY OF PEACE

⌂ PRIME MINISTER    ◇ SHARON

"'Sharon,' 'Arafat,' and 'Bush' are all encoded together by name in the Torah, with both Biblical expressions of the ultimate time of danger, the 'End of Days.'

"And while there are many interpretations of the meaning of the 'End of Days,' all scholars agree it suggests a danger as least as great as the plain text of the Book of Daniel states:

"'And there shall be a time of trouble such as never was since there was a nation.'"

"If we're talking about Israel, that's saying a lot," said Omri, getting up to leave.

————————————————

I think the real problem is not that Sharon won't believe in the Bible code, but that he does not want to make peace.

What persuaded me of that was not my meeting with his son, but my meeting with an old friend at the Ministry of Defense, the chief scientist General Isaac Ben-Israel.

I had known Isaac for ten years. I had warned him that the Bible code said Rabin would be killed at the same time I warned Rabin, a year in advance. I had taken Dr. Rips to the military headquarters in Tel Aviv, to the Kirya, to meet with him. Isaac, a physicist who decided what weapons Israel would make and buy, was the only man in the Israeli government with a strong enough scientific background to understand the Bible code on the level Rips could explain it.

Because he understood, and because he had seen the Rabin prediction come true, Isaac had never been afraid to tell anyone the warnings I passed on to him. He told other generals, he told all the intelligence chiefs, he even spoke to at least one Prime Minister.

But now, at our meeting in Tel Aviv, in April 2001, Isaac scared me. We had never really discussed politics. I just assumed he was on the left, aligned with Rabin, Peres, and Barak.

Now, General Ben-Israel seemed to be reflecting the attitude of the new Sharon administration.

I knew he met weekly with all the top defense officials, sometimes including the Prime Minister. And his position had hardened.

I showed Isaac all the same code tables I had shown Omri, and hoped to show Sharon. I especially emphasized the table where "Sharon" and "Arafat" and "Bush" all appeared with "End of Days." I said what I told everyone, that according to the code, the only choice appeared to be peace or annihilation.

"What can Arafat do to us?" demanded Ben-Israel. "Arafat can't hurt us."

"Of course you can defeat him militarily," I said. "But if you do the world will condemn you, and the Islamic lunatics with missiles and unconventional weapons will attack you."

"I don't think the world will condemn us," said Ben-Israel. "Not if it follows a major terrorist attack."

"What do you call major?" I asked.

"Not three dead, but three hundred," said Isaac. "We've stopped them several times, plotting to blow up an office building in Tel Aviv. Something like that."

"What would Israel then do?" I asked.

"Something devastating," said Isaac.

He was not willing to share details. But it was obvious that he was repeating contingency plans that had already been made at the highest military and intelligence circles.

And I knew in that moment that Sharon was just waiting for an excuse to take decisive military action against the Palestinians. It was already planned.

I told Isaac that I was afraid it would be a disaster for Israel, that it would inevitably bring exactly the kind of response the Bible code warned of—the ultimate danger that the code stated Israel would face within the next five years.

"We could survive a chemical attack," said Ben-Israel. "We've already contemplated that. Perhaps 12,000 would die. It would be tragic, but it would not be terminal."

I showed Isaac a code table. "Arafat" was crossed by "plague," and the full verse in the plain text of the Bible stated "the dead in the plague were 14,700."

○ ARAFAT ◇ PLAGUE □ THE DEAD IN THE PLAGUE WERE 14,700

"What about an atomic attack?" I asked.

"That could be terminal," said Isaac.

I left that meeting more shaken than by any meeting I had with any Israeli official. And everything that followed in the next few days, Israel's bombing of the Syrian radar station in Lebanon, Israel's invasion of Gaza, all clearly timed to prevent the Jordanians from presenting Sharon with a peace proposal, made it clear to me that the Prime Minister was waiting for the moment he could fulfill his destiny—the moment he could strike the Palestinians with full military force.

What was encoded in the Bible never looked more real to me. It was not enough that Arafat appeared to accept the code's warnings. I also had to get through to Sharon. I had to scare him the same way I scared Arafat.

I had to convince Sharon that this really was the "End of Days."

As I said goodbye to my friend Isaac, I asked him who could get me to Sharon. He suggested that I go see a retired general the Prime Minister planned to make the new chief of the Mossad.

---

"I've heard rumors that you'll be the next chief of the Mossad," I told General Meir Dagan when we met in Rosh Pina, the town where he lived in northern Israel.

"I've heard those same rumors," Dagan replied.

I had come north to see the right-wing general, because after Omri he was the Prime Minister's most trusted confidant. After Sharon stormed Temple Mount, Dagan was a lead speaker at an antipeace rally in Jerusalem. "We must respond with war for war," Dagan told the crowd. "The time has come to send Yasir Arafat back to Tunisia," the North African country where he lived in exile.

It was this man I had to persuade that Israel had no alternative but peace, because the only other choice was annihilation.

I showed Dagan the same code tables I had shown Omri, where "Sharon" and "Arafat" appeared with the "End of Days," and also the warnings of "atomic holocaust" and "World War" in 2006.

"So what does it all mean?" asked Dagan. "And what can we do?"

"I think it means that Israel is in terminal danger, and that you have five years to find a way to survive," I said. "But I'm certain that the future can be changed. That's why I've come to see you."

I knew that Dagan was totally secular. I asked him if he could take the Bible code seriously.

"Yes," he said, "because if the danger is real, it's not something we can ignore."

Dagan had been in charge of counter-terrorism the last time the right wing was in power, when Bibi Netanyahu was Prime Minister. I told him that I had noticed that people with an intelligence background were more open to the Bible code, even if they were not religious.

"You're right," said Dagan. "We have to be. We can't ignore any warning."

But there was something more, something that Dagan did not reveal to me until we met again months later.

It was in December 2001. Sharon had just named Dagan to lead the Israeli team in the cease-fire talks with the Palestinians, to be mediated by the U.S. special envoy, General Anthony Zinni.

Everyone knew that Sharon had named Dagan to make sure there would be no peace agreement. But again, Dagan surprised me with his willingness to persuade the Prime Minister to meet with me to discuss the warnings in the Bible code.

I showed him the Bible code tables that foretold 9/11, the attack on "Twin Towers" encoded with "airplane," and I told him that the code seemed to warn that Israel, too, faced terror attacks on a completely different scale.

"I'll talk to the Prime Minister and I'll talk to Omri," said Dagan, "but Sharon certainly won't meet with you now."

Israel was in a state of yet greater crisis. Three major terrorist attacks had claimed the lives of twenty-five just in the past few days, and now Israeli fighter jets were attacking Gaza and the West Bank.

"I understand the moment," I told Dagan. "But what's going on now is a sideshow. Twenty-five dead is a tragedy, but if the code is right, the real dangers lie ahead, and thousands will die, and then tens of thousands, and finally your entire country will face annihilation."

Dagan was silent. I knew that he was a tough combat general, but I wondered if I had gone too far.

"I hate to state it so harshly," I said. "And if we had more time I would say the same thing more gently. But I've been trying to get through to the Prime Minister for months, and I want you to understand and tell him that we're talking about the survival of your country."

"I promised you I would talk to Sharon, and I will," said Dagan. "I'm not religious, but I do believe there are supernatural forces that affect events here."

I was shocked. I knew from my first meeting with Dagan that he was open-minded about the Bible code. Now, I knew why.

"From personal experience?" I asked.

"Yes," said Dagan, but he did not explain.

I decided not to probe further. But I wondered what this tough right-wing general had experienced to cause him to believe in supernatural forces, and therefore to accept the potential reality of a code in the Bible that reveals the future.

"I believe something like this can be real, that it can be true," said Dagan. It was enough for me.

My goal was to sit face to face with Ariel Sharon, as I had sat face to face with Yasir Arafat.

I told Dagan that I might see Arafat again.

"Don't go in the next few days," he said.

"I'm not afraid," I replied.

"Don't go now," said Dagan.

A few days later, after another terrorist attack, Israeli helicopter gunships struck Arafat's compound in the West Bank city of Ramallah and Israeli tanks surrounded Arafat's office.

The Palestinian leader would be kept prisoner there for months to come.

Meir Dagan would, in fact, be named Chief of the Mossad in September 2002 by his old friend, the Prime Minister Ariel Sharon.

---

The picture on the wall was like a time capsule. Yasir Arafat shaking hands with Yitzhak Rabin on the White House lawn, with Bill Clinton hovering over them. Shimon Peres stood at Rabin's side.

I had just entered Peres's office at the Foreign Ministry in Tel Aviv. But the peace he more than anyone had championed now seemed a distant, sad memory.

I was immediately taken in to see Peres.

He was the last hope, but he looked old and tired and depressed. He seemed to feel the loss more than anyone, perhaps because he more than anyone had created the moment captured in that photograph.

I had last seen Peres when he was Prime Minister, in late January 1996, just months after the Rabin assassination. Now Peres was the left-wing counterweight in the coalition government led by Sharon.

I showed him the same Bible code tables I had shown Omri and Dagan, where the "End of Days" and "World War" and "atomic holocaust" all appeared with 2006.

"When I first saw you," said Peres, "the danger was ten years away. Now it's only five years, and it doesn't seem so unlikely anymore."

After the failure of Camp David, after nearly seven months of the new Intifada, after the election of Sharon, the same things I feared to tell Peres when he was Prime Minister, because they sounded so Apocalyptic, were now ordinary common sense. But I told Peres that perhaps there was hope.

"I just met with Arafat, and he seems to accept without question the warnings in the Bible code," I said.

Peres wanted all the details. "What did you tell him, and how did he react?" he asked.

"I told him that according to the code, his real choice was not peace or street riots, or even peace or war, but peace or annihilation. He seemed to accept it completely."

I opened my book again to the Bible code illustration that showed the two expressions of the "End of Days," and circled the Hebrew letters that spelled "A-R-A-F-A-T."

"And how did he react?" asked Peres.

"He didn't seem surprised," I said. "He told me that he already believed we are living in critical times, but when he realized the Hebrew expression was the same as in Arabic—that the 'End of Days' was said exactly the same way in both languages, it shook him. He repeated it to all of his aides, and they all seemed shaken by it."

○ THE END OF DAYS   □ IN THE THE END OF DAYS   ◇ ARAFAT

"If it's predicted, what can we do?" asked Peres.

It was the same question he had asked me when we met five years earlier, when I showed him that "atomic holocaust" was encoded with 2006.

"Arafat asked me the same question," I said. "Except he asked 'If it's written, what can we do?'"

"That's what the Arabs say," Peres noted. "'It is written.' They think everything is predetermined."

"I tried to persuade him that the future can be changed, that what's encoded in the Bible is a warning, not a prediction," I told Peres. "What we do, what you do, what he does, will determine what actually happens."

I also told Peres that I was in contact with Sharon through his son Omri, but that I did not think Sharon wanted to make peace.

Peres did not protest. He did not defend Sharon. He just said, "I already believed we have no choice but to make peace, so why are you telling me all this?"

"Because Arafat's total belief in the Bible code, his complete acceptance of its warnings, may give you an entirely new opening—even if you can't fully believe there's a code in the Bible that predicts the future."

"He and I are from different worlds," said Peres. "Arafat is a primitive, from a culture that is still basically agricultural. I'm from a culture that is scientific, democratic. It's so different. It's so difficult to communicate."

Peres was silent for a moment. His sadness was palpable.

He was without question the smartest Israeli politician I had met. Everyone dismissed him as a dreamer, and said Sharon was the realist. But I had exactly the opposite impression. Sharon was the dreamer. He still believed he could win a military victory, settle everything with a tank battle. Peres was the realist. He knew that the code was right, that the Arabs would soon have nuclear weapons, that Israel had five years to find a way to survive.

# CHAPTER EIGHT

# CODE OF LIFE

All life on this planet came from a code. It was imprinted in a single DNA molecule. But no one knows where that code came from.

Early in my search for the key to the Bible code, I may have also stumbled onto the key to the code of life.

The secret of the genetic code is revealed in Genesis, where God tells Abraham: "I will bless thee greatly, and I will greatly multiply thy seed as the stars of Heaven, and as the sand that is upon the seashore; and in thy seed shall all the nations of the world be blessed."

Hidden in those famous words is the true story of our Creation. According to the Bible code, our "DNA was brought in a vehicle."

○ DNA WAS BROUGHT IN A VEHICLE  □ YOUR SEED  ◇ IN A VEHICLE YOUR SEED

"Your seed" crosses "DNA was brought in a vehicle." "In a vehicle, your seed, all the people of the Earth," is stated again in the hidden text of the Bible, where God says, "In thy seed shall all the nations of the world be blessed."

When I found that encoded in the Bible, I couldn't believe it. It seemed like science fiction. DNA, the molecule of life, sent to Earth in a spaceship.

I wondered if any reputable scientist would even consider such a fantastic idea.

I called the most eminent authority in the world, Francis Crick, the Nobel laureate biologist who discovered the double helix, the spiral structure of DNA. It was one of the greatest scientific discoveries of all time. As Crick himself declared in the first moment of revelation, "We've discovered the secret of life."

"Is it possible," I asked Crick, when I reached him at the Salk Institute in San Diego, California, "that our DNA came from another planet?"

"I published that theory twenty-five years ago," said Crick. "I called it 'Directed Panspermia.'"

"Do you think it arrived in a meteor or comet?" I asked.

"No," said Crick. "Anything living would have died in such an accidental journey through space."

"Are you saying that DNA was sent here in a vehicle?" I asked.

"It's the only possibility," said Crick.

Crick had just confirmed the Bible code's statement of the origin of life on Earth. But I did not mention the Bible code to him. Crick is defiantly secular. Instead I asked him to explain his theory of the genesis of DNA.

The DNA molecule, Crick said, was far too complex to have evolved spontaneously on Earth in the short time between the formation of this planet 4 billion years ago and the first appearance of life 3.8 billion years ago.

"But it is unlikely," said Crick, "that living organisms could have reached Earth as spores from another star, or embedded in a meteorite."

Therefore, said Crick, there was only one possibility:

"A primitive form of life was planted on the Earth by an advanced civilization on another planet—deliberately."

It was extraordinary. Crick was telling me exactly what the Bible code stated—"DNA was brought in a vehicle."

Crick said that our DNA was intentionally sent here in a "spaceship" and that "all life on Earth represents a clone derived from a single extraterrestrial organism." He stated it explicitly when he first published his theory in 1973.

Now I asked him if he still believed in "Directed Panspermia."

"We know very little about the origins of life," said Crick, "but all of the new scientific discoveries support my theory, and none disprove it."

"There has been one big change since our theory was first published," he told me. "We now know that other stars do have planets. So it certainly is possible that an advanced technological civilization existed elsewhere in the galaxy even before the Earth was formed."

Crick was more certain than ever. "DNA was sent here in a vehicle," he said. "By aliens."

———————————————

It wasn't exactly the story told in Genesis. But it was clearly stated in the Bible code.

I wondered what Eli Rips, the scientist who discovered the code, would say about this theory of our true origins. Would it conflict with his religious beliefs, with his faith in the plain words of the Bible, which of course say that God created man and all other life on Earth?

In November 1998, when I arrived in the Middle East to launch my search for the obelisks, for the hidden key to the Bible code, I showed Rips what the Bible code said about the code of life—"DNA was brought in a vehicle."

"It's an extraordinary match," said Rips. "'DNA in a vehicle' and 'your seed in a vehicle'—it's perfect, it's self-referential."

I told Rips what Crick had told me, and had written 25 years ago.

"It's different from Creation theory only in one way—by renaming the intelligent agent," said Rips. "Evolution of DNA on Earth is not realistic, so an extraneous agent brought it here. Dr. Crick just refrains from calling the hero by name."

Rips, who never sees a conflict between science and religion, who believes that both are searches for ultimate truth and must lead to the same place, was excited about this find.

Encouraged, I showed Eli related encodings. "Genetic code" appeared in the Bible with "his gene you will inherit." Rips found "to advance man" encoded in the same place.

O GENETIC CODE   ◇ HIS GENE YOU WILL INHERIT   □ TO ADVANCE MAN

"DNA spiral" was also encoded in the Bible, and crossing that in the hidden text were the words "in Adam the model, template." "From a code" appeared on the same table.

"It's a very good meeting with a clear and simple statement of the meaning of the encoding," said Rips. "And the odds against 'DNA spiral' appearing at all are 300 to 1."

I asked Rips whether he thought it was possible that both the Bible code and the DNA code had the same double helix structure, that both were two spirals intertwined—that there was perhaps just one universal code.

Finally, I showed him that the two codes—"DNA code" and "Bible code"—appeared together against very high odds, that both were encoded in the same place in the Bible.

○ DNA SPIRAL    □ IN ADAM THE MODEL, TEMPLATE    ◇ FROM A CODE

○ DNA CODE    □ BIBLE CODE

Rips was very excited. He disappeared for a few moments to his study, and came back with a Bible code table printed out on a transparency. It showed "Judgment of God" and "Mercy of God" encoded in the same place.

Rips took the flat transparency and joined the ends together, turning it into a cylinder.

The two strands, "Judgment" and "Mercy," were intertwined around each other.

O MERCY OF GOD     ◇ JUDGMENT OF GOD

"We've always been looking at a three-dimensional cylinder," explained Rips. "We just unroll it to display the code in two dimensions on a computer screen, just like you lay a map out flat instead of showing the globe. But look what happens when we turn it back into a cylinder."

"Mercy of God" was clearly intertwined around "Judgment of God," the two faces of the Almighty were presented in exactly the same form as the two strands of DNA.

"It's a double helix," said Rips. "Both codes, the code of life and the code of the Torah, may have the same structure. And truly neither arose here on Earth."

---

"The roots of our form of life go back to another place in the universe, almost certainly another planet," wrote Crick, expanding on his theory of Directed Panspermia.

"It had reached a very advanced form there before anything much had started here. And life here was seeded by microorganisms sent in some form of spaceship by an advanced civilization."

As evidence, Crick suggested two things: (1) "The genetic code is identical in all living things"; (2) "The earliest organisms appear suddenly, without any sign of more simple precursors here on Earth."

"We shall postulate that on some distant planet, some 4 billion or so years ago, there had evolved a form of higher creature, who like ourselves had discovered science and technology, developing them far beyond anything we have accomplished," wrote Crick.

"They would have known that in the long run, their own civilization was doomed. Of course, there may have been reasons for them to believe they could not even survive in the short run. Without doubt, they would have planned to colonize neighboring planets.

"Once the scale and the nature of the galaxy is appreciated it is intolerable not to know whether we are its sole inhabitants," said Crick. "It may even be very dangerous not to do so."

Finally, Crick asked the big question that still haunts us: "Are the senders or their descendants still alive? Or have the hazards of 4 billion years been too much for them?"

---

DNA is a language. It is written with four letters.

"The filament of DNA is information, a message written in a code of chemicals, one chemical for each letter," explains Matt Ridley in his book

*Genome*, which tells the story of the newly decoded human blueprint.

"It is almost too good to be true," notes Ridley, "but the code turns out to be written in a way we can understand. Just like written English, the genetic code is a linear language, written in a straight line."

It was the same startling discovery that Dr. Rips had made about the Bible code. It was intended for us, written in a language we could understand—as the code itself said, where "code key" appeared, it was "in our hands to solve."

The DNA code, like the Bible code "existed in the language of man."

Was it possible that our search for the "code key" might also lead to some universal code, to the code of life, to the code of all Creation?

I discovered that on the original table, the code finding that led to my entire quest, where "Mouth of the Obelisks" crossed "Code Key," there was another extraordinary revelation.

Also encoded in the same place were the words "family tree in Lisan." It could also be translated "he will trace the origins of the ancestors in Lisan."

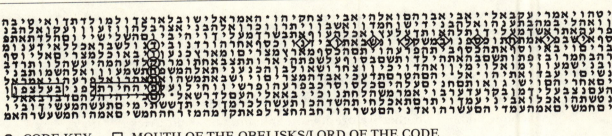

○ CODE KEY    □ MOUTH OF THE OBELISKS/LORD OF THE CODE
◇ FAMILY TREE IN LISAN/HE WILL TRACE ORIGIN OF ANCESTORS IN LISAN

It clearly connected the Bible code to the genetic code, and both to the same location, and suggested that the "Lord of the Code" was not merely the Encoder, but also our Creator.

"In Lisan DNA" was also encoded in the Bible. In Hebrew "Lisan" also means "language," so the same words can be translated "in the language of DNA." And that was crossed by "a copy of everything was brought."

שׁ א ס י צ ע ה ל ע ה ה ב ז מ ה נ ה כ ה ו ה ת א ר י ק ט ה ו ל י ב ד
שׁ א ר ל ע ת נ פ נ ה מ ת ה מ א ס ש י ו ס י מ ת ה ת א ו ס י ר י ה ת
ע ב ק נ ת ה ה ה ש פ א ל ה נ ה ו י ע י (ב) ש ה ס י ו ב ק ב ת ה נ ה ת א ן
מ א ו ה ש ה ת א ה ת כ ר נ י ו י ה י ו (ל) ה ת א נ י ל ע ש י א ב ן
ן ה כ ל י י ה י ו י ד ש י ק ס ם כ ב ע י ל ש ל ע י ו ה י י ו
צ ר א ה ת ז ח ת א ו ל ר ש א ל ו ת מ א ה נ ה ק ר ש ל א ה ד ה ש ב ו
ה א ב ד ד ב ע ל א ב צ ל [א][ב][ה][ל][כ][ה][נ][ש] ס י ש מ ה ו ן ח ע ו ד י ע ל
י ה ל ת ה א ת ח א ק י ו א ת י ש ת (ד) ק ה י ר י צ מ א ר ב ר י
ו ה י י ש ל ע ל ע ו י נ ג י ל ע ת נ ו א ב (ו) י ע פ ק ה ק נ י ה ל א ק
י ו ת ה מ ו י ל א ו ל ל ח ת א ל ל ר (א) ש י י ב י ש ד ת ק א ת ו
ס ה מ י ס ל ז י ו מ י י ל ע ס ו ז ר כ א ה ו י ה י ע נ ט נ ל כ ר ה כ
ב ס י נ ק נ ה מ ר נ ה ת ה ל ע ד ל ב מ ל כ ד ה ת א כ ט א ת ה י ר ע
ן ר י ר ה י ו ה ב ג ו ד ה ד ק ת ר נ כ י ס פ ת כ ל ה ה מ נ

○ IN LISAN DNA/IN THE LANGUAGE OF DNA  □ A COPY OF EVERYTHING WAS BROUGHT

It was like a high-tech Noah's Ark, with each life form preserved in DNA code. "In Lisan DNA" appeared a second time, and "Mazra" appeared in the same place.

ה ו י א ו י ה ה ח נ ג מ ה ת נ ב ל ה י ל ע ת מ ש ו ן מ ש ה י ל ע ת ת נ ו
ל כ ב ה ר ה ה ט י מ ד ב ש ה מ י מ י ת ש ל ש ו ס י ו י ש ל ה כ ל
י ת מ ש י ה ת ת א נ ה י ת ל ת (ב) ל ד ל מ ל ע מ ו ת ד ז מ [ע][ר][ז][מ] ו ת ב א ו
ק פ א ל ת ר ש י ב א צ א צ (ל) כ ה ל ע מ ו נ ו ה צ ר ס פ י ר ש ע ן ב
מ ג ב ל א י ש י ע י ע (ש) ה ת ה ס ו ב ר י ה צ ת ה ל ב א א
ה כ ל י ש ר י ו מ מ ש ה א (ו) ה י א נ ג י ב ל ו מ ק י י ל ב א ן א
ש ב מ ת ה כ ה ו ו ר ה ו א ה (כ) נ ש מ ש ב ה ת ע ה ת ש ר ב ג ת ה נ א ר א
ש ת ת ד ת א ל ת ד י ו ה ר ה ו (ד) מ ש ו ב ה ל י א צ ת ב מ צ ר ת ר מ י א ׳
י ה ת ד ב ת ל ל כ ל ת ל י ר (ו) ל ו א ה י ר י ד ר א ז ר ת ר א ד ת נ
ו ל ש א ה ת ס א ה נ ח צ ו ה ת ה ט י ו ב ה ת א ה ד ל א א צ י ו י ה ב ׳
ר ת ל מ נ כ א ס נ ג ת ת ש ו ב ה י י ת ת מ ה ה מ י ת ל מ ר

○ IN LISAN DNA  □ MAZRA/SEEDED

In Hebrew, "Mazra" also means "seeded," again a perfect description of how Crick, and the Bible code, said life arrived on our planet.

And in the same place appeared the same verse from Genesis that also appeared with "DNA was brought in a vehicle," God's promise to Abraham: "I will greatly multiply thy seed as the stars of Heaven."

"Code of Life" was also encoded, again with "Mazra," again with "seeded."

O CODE OF LIFE    □ MAZRA/SEEDED

Again and again the ✕ on the treasure map, "Mazra" and "Lisan" appeared with "DNA" just as the same two locations appeared with everything related to the "Bible code."

"DNA spiral" was in fact encoded with "Mazra" and "Lisan, tongue of sea."

And again the code clearly stated that the genetic code would also be found on an "obelisk." "On obelisk" in fact crossed "DNA code."

"Human DNA" also appeared with "obelisk," and the hidden text stated "copy on a pillar."

"Creation of Man" is encoded twice, once with "Lisan," and once with "Mazra." "This is the solution" appears in the original words of the Bible, overlapping "Lisan," where the location is encoded with "Creation of Man."

"I gave it to you as an inheritance, I am God," are the words in the plain text crossing "Creation of Man," where it is encoded with "Mazra."

○ DNA SPIRAL   □ FROM A CODE   ◇ ANCIENT KEY   □ LISAN, TONGUE OF SEA
⬠ MAZRA

○ DNA CODE   □ ON OBELISK   ◇ IN ADAM THE TEMPLATE, MODEL

O HUMAN DNA   ◇ OBELISK   □ COPY ON A PILLAR

O CREATION OF MAN   ◇ LISAN   □ THIS IS THE SOLUTION

O CREATION OF MAN  ◇ MAZRA/SEEDED

□ I GAVE IT TO YOU AS AN INHERITANCE, I AM GOD

It is an extraordinarily clear statement that the key to the code of life, as well as the Bible code, may lie buried in the peninsula whose name means "language," at the bay whose name means "seeded."

It also seemed a very clear statement that the Bible code and the genetic code must therefore have a common source—that the same alien brought both to Earth.

# CHAPTER NINE

# INVASION

Every time I returned to the Middle East it felt more like the End of Days.

On Good Friday, March 29, 2002, on Easter and Passover in the Holy Land, Israeli Prime Minister Ariel Sharon sent 60 tanks, 200 armored personnel carriers and 2500 soldiers into Yasir Arafat's compound in Ramallah, in retaliation for a week of suicide bombings.

Military bulldozers crashed through the walls of the Palestinian leader's headquarters, and Israeli troops seized all but a few rooms, making Arafat a prisoner in the same place where I had met with him a year earlier.

Israel occupied nearly every major city in the West Bank, in the biggest offensive since the 1967 Six-Day War.

It was all foreseen. "Sharon is invading" crossed "Arafat" in the Bible Code.

O SHARON IS INVADING   □ ARAFAT

I had found that prediction nearly a year before the attack, and even the time was foretold. "Sharon invaded" appeared again, crossed by "Passover."

○ SHARON INVADED    □ PASSOVER

And, most ominously, "Sharon invaded" appeared again with "war" and "in the End of Days."

○ SHARON INVADED    □ IN THE END OF DAYS    ◇ WAR

Now it had all come true.

Arafat and Sharon were fulfilling each other's destinies. Arafat had put Sharon in office by rejecting the peace plan offered by Barak and Clinton at Camp David. Now Sharon, by invading Palestine and surrounding Arafat's compound in Ramallah, had made Arafat a martyr, a hero to the entire Arab world.

While the battle raged across the West Bank, I sat with Eli Rips at his home in Jerusalem. We looked at the codes.

Rips typed in the name of the Israeli military operation, "Defensive Wall." It appeared once in the Bible code, crossed by the name of the Palestinian city where the heaviest fighting was right now flattening a refugee camp, "Jenin." Just below that "Casbah" also appeared. It was the name of the old city in Nablus, where the other fierce battle raged.

O DEFENSIVE WALL    □ JENIN    △ CASBAH    □ THE OVERTHROW OF THE CITIES

The plain text crossing "Defensive Wall" spoke of "the overthrow of the cities." Just above that was encoded "fighting." And also in the same place the original words of the Bible captured the moment: "They hated, and they could not speak of peace."

It was as detailed and accurate as the news reports on CNN, as precise as the headlines in the *Jerusalem Post* and the *New York Times,* encoded in a text that was 3000 years old.

Rips calculated the odds. Just the match between the names of the cities and the name of the military operation was several hundred thousand to one beyond chance.

"This is the same report I saw on television last night," I told Rips. "Where do you think it will end?"

"I think Israel will again find itself with its back against the sea, like the ancient Israelites did on the shores of the Red Sea," said the mathematician.

I understood the allusion. Rips was talking about the moment recorded in the Bible, on the first Passover 3200 years ago, when the Hebrews fleeing Egypt found themselves trapped between the Pharaoh's onrushing army and the waters of the Red Sea, facing certain annihilation.

"We will again need Divine intervention," said Rips.

Rips understood that while Israel now had the upper hand, the battle had barely begun. I feared he was right, but I could not imagine anyone now parting the waters.

If there was to be a miracle this time, it was perhaps the miracle we were witnessing, the details of modern events encoded in an ancient text, and a warning of what was yet to come.

---

"Everything that's happening now is only a sideshow," I told General Meir Dagan, the man considered by many closest to Sharon, a former chief of counterintelligence who the Prime Minister was soon to make the new chief of the Mossad.

I showed Dagan the remarkably accurate prediction of the current warfare, and told him that he must warn Sharon that according to the code, this was quite literally the "End of Days," and that Israel faced annihilation.

"I have already given the Prime Minister your letter," said Dagan, "but I don't know if he read it."

"You must tell him that it all keeps coming true," I said.

"You remind me of a story told by the Greek poet Homer," said Dagan. "The story of Cassandra, who was cursed to know the future, but never to be believed."

I handed him a new letter for Sharon. It repeated the warning I had been trying to get to the Prime Minister for a full year.

"This critical moment in Israel's history was without doubt clearly foreseen," my letter stated. "'Sharon,' 'Arafat,' and 'Bush' are all encoded together by name in the Torah, with the ultimate time of great danger—'End of Days.'"

Now I added a new warning: "If the code is right, what is happening now is only a sideshow. The real danger lies ahead. First, a 'plague,' an attack with chemical or biological weapons, in which tens of thousands may die. Finally, an 'atomic holocaust.'"

Dagan promised he would again get my letter to Sharon, through the Prime Minister's Chief of Staff, Uri Shani. "He's the man closest to Sharon on a day-to-day basis, even closer than Omri," said Dagan, referring to the Prime Minister's son, who I had met with a year before.

Within a few days, Sharon's chief of staff agreed to meet with me, but only after the Prime Minister had finished his meetings with the U.S. Secretary of State, Colin Powell, who had just arrived in Israel to negotiate a cease-fire between the Israelis and the Palestinians.

---

So I went instead to see the one Palestinian leader who was not held prisoner, in the one city in the West Bank that had not yet been invaded, the oldest city in the world, Jericho.

Saeb Erekat, the Palestinians' chief peace negotiator, remembered our meeting a year before. He had translated for me and Arafat when we met at the same compound in Ramallah that was now battered and surrounded by tanks.

I handed Erekat a new letter for Arafat, but before he could read it, the Palestinian leader called Erekat. Arafat said he was cold, running out of food, fuel, and medicine, and worried that Powell would not see him because there had just been a new suicide bombing in Jerusalem.

Nonetheless, after a quick call to the American Embassy, Erekat read my letter. It stated:

"I am back in the Middle East now to warn both you and the Israelis that this is the time foreseen by all three major Western religions—the 'End of Days'—a time of danger greater than the world has ever faced.

"This may be your last chance to make peace, and avoid the horror yet to come. The fate of both the Israelis and Palestinians will be the same. If you don't make peace, you will face the 'End of Days' together. Now you must act. This is the moment."

Erekat read my letter carefully, and said he would give it to Arafat when they met with Colin Powell.

"When is the 'End of Days?'" Erekat asked. "Now?"

"Right now," I said. "It's already begun."

"What the Israelis are doing will bring the whole world to an end?" asked Erekat.

"What you are doing to each other," I said.

I showed him the code tables I had shown Dagan, where "Sharon is invading" crossed "Arafat" and appeared again with "in the End of Days."

I also showed Erekat another table, where "World War" was encoded with "terrorism," and the Arabic word for "suicide bomber," "Shahid," appeared in the same place.

"It says 'Shahid' there?" asked Erekat, now very intent on the Hebrew characters.

I pointed to the word, and repeated to him a part of my letter to Arafat. "That's why I said this to Arafat: 'You must rise above your battle with Sharon. Terrorists are your mutual enemy, and if empowered will kill both of you, destroy both of your peoples, and finally all human civilization.'"

Erekat again promised he would give my letter to Arafat, and arrange for us to meet—if Powell could persuade the Israelis to lift their siege.

As I drove back through the Israeli military checkpoint, I wondered again if I had gone too far. Erekat had taken me very seriously, Arafat believed me absolutely, and Dagan was really trying to warn Sharon that a code in the Bible said the Apocalypse was right upon us.

It still seemed to me unreal. And yet the warning I had been sounding to world leaders from the Bible code for years, the warning I could barely believe myself, had by now become common wisdom.

Even before a month of suicide bombings had killed 150 Israelis, even before Sharon started waging all-out war against the Palestinians, *New York Times* columnist Tom Friedman sounded nearly the same warning.

Friedman said in the *Times* exactly what I had tried to tell every Israeli Prime Minister since Rabin had been assassinated, what I had been trying to tell the White House since Camp David, that the conflict in the Middle East "is starting to feel like the fuse for a much larger war of civilizations."

He warned, as I had just again tried to warn Sharon, that "weapons of mass destruction" in the hands of terrorists or radical Arab states might "wipe Israel off the map."

The spread of nuclear and biological weapons, the rise of bin Laden, the growing link between religious fanatics and terrorists, had made what seemed paranoid and Apocalyptic just a few years ago almost ordinary common sense today. The world had caught up with the Bible code.

And it never felt more so—at least not since I watched the World Trade Towers fall—than it seemed today, as I drove past the military checkpoint out of Jericho.

I had seen it coming since Yitzhak Rabin was killed. Where "assassin will assassinate" crossed "Yizhak Rabin," right above those words was a warning: "All his people to war."

○ YITZHAK RABIN   □ ASSASSIN WILL ASSASSINATE   ◇ ALL HIS PEOPLE TO WAR

The murder of the Prime Minister who made peace with Arafat was not just a turning point for Israel, but for the world.

I had met with Rabin's daughter, Dalia, on my last trip to Israel. "It's already started," she said as we sat down to talk at the Knesset, Israel's parliament. "I tried to stop it from happening, but nobody would listen. He's doing it right now."

I didn't understand. "Sharon," she said. "The attack is already under way." Later, on CNN, I saw what she meant—Sharon had sent F-16s and helicopter gunships and tanks into Gaza and the West Bank, the beginning of the biggest Israeli assault on the territories since Rabin and Arafat shook hands at the Oslo accords in 1993.

Dalia Rabin knew in that instant that the peace her father had made was dead. She was now Deputy Defense Minister, and had just come from a Cabinet meeting. "I tried to stop it," she repeated, "but nobody would listen."

I gave her a copy of the letter I had sent her father more than a year before he was killed in November 1995, warning him that the Bible code predicted he would be assassinated. She read it without saying a word. It clearly shook her deeply.

The memory of that awful moment, combined with her horror at what was happening at this moment, was so clear on her face that I didn't want to go further. But she was not only Rabin's daughter. She was also an important government official, and I wanted her to understand the far greater dangers Israel still faced.

"If the code is right, what has happened and what is happening now is only the beginning," I told her.

That was four months before Sharon invaded the West Bank full force, an invasion I knew was predicted in the Bible. But it was the greater warnings that were on my mind — the warnings of a "plague" that were encoded with 2005, and the warnings of "World War" and "atomic holocaust" that were encoded with 2006.

"I believe the dangers are real, even without the code," said Dalia Rabin. "I'm trying to restrain Sharon and we're preparing for chemical and biological and atomic attacks."

She was silent for a moment. "If it's predicted, what can we do?" she asked.

"Peres and Arafat both asked me the same question," I told her. "I don't think it's a prediction, but a warning, and what we do determines what actually happens."

She gestured to my book that was lying on the table, with the code's prediction of her father's assassination on the cover, and the letter that I wrote the Prime Minister a year earlier that was lying beneath it.

"You couldn't stop that," she said.

"I think we could have," I told her. "Your father received the warning, but he didn't believe it."

She was silent again for a moment. She looked so sad. "They're bombing Gaza right now," she said. "What can we do?"

"I'll tell you what I told Arafat and what I'm trying to tell Sharon—I don't think there will be peace until both sides understand that the alternative is annihilation. I think Arafat believes me, but I haven't been able to sit down with Sharon."

"He won't listen to you," she said. "He doesn't want to hear it. Maybe things have to get much worse before anyone will listen."

---

As I waited to see if I could get through to Sharon, and if he would allow me to meet with his prisoner Arafat, I went to see the general in perhaps the most critical position in Israeli intelligence.

General Yossi Kuperwasser was in charge of intelligence analysis. All the information gathered by all of Israel's intelligence agencies, from spies, from satellites, from the Americans and the Europeans, came to his desk.

On Monday, April 15, 2002, I met with him at the Kirya, the walled, tightly guarded Israeli military headquarters in the heart of Tel Aviv.

"You shaved your beard," said General Kuperwasser when I entered his office. At first I couldn't imagine what he was talking about. Then I realized that we had met before—on my first trip to Israel ten years earlier, when I came to talk to the chief of Israeli intelligence about the future of warfare.

Kuperwasser was then a young assistant to the general in charge. I had only known him as Yossi, and never made the connection. Everything had come full circle. It was on the way out of that meeting ten years ago that I had first learned by chance about the Bible code.

Kuperwasser did not have to be convinced. Although he was not religious, he already took the Bible code seriously.

"I was at the airport years ago, looking for something to read, and I saw your book," he told me. "We have to pay attention to any warning of existential danger."

Our mutual friend, the chief scientist at the Ministry of Defense, General Isaac Ben-Israel, had already briefed Kuperwasser about the new warnings in the Bible code.

Now I showed him the code tables. "'Smallpox' is encoded with '2005,'" I told the general.

ו ה י ד י ו ס ע ב ה ר ח ר ח · ו ה י י א ו ת ר כ י ס ר ט ס ה י ש נ י ש ו
ם ם ו י ה י ה ג נ פ ל ד ה ה ⓐ ו ג ע מ ע ב ו ה ס ה ל ע ד ע ז
א צ ה ו ת א ו ב י ר ק ו ת ⓑ ש ה ס י ו ס י ס צ ע ש ש ק ש י
ל מ [ת ו א מ ע ב ש ו ר ל א ר ש ע ה ה ב ר א ה פ ג מ ב ס י מ ה ה] ו
ר ש ב צ ח ו ר י ס ב ו ג ⓑ ס ב כ ה ת א ף ר ו ה ס ו ר ע ה
ש מ ר ד ז ח ו נ ח ו י ו ⓢ נ ס ם ש מ ו ש ה ר ח ה מ מ ז ב א
י ד ל מ ל א ס ע מ ר א י ⓘ י ת י י ת ה ה ת ו א י ו ת ג ר ה
ד מ צ י ו ו ה י ה ל א ל ו ⓣ ש ו ו ע ל כ א י י ה · ל
ל ו י ל ת ל נ ב ה ר ת ◈ר ל ◈ ם ר פ ◈ מ ב ל נ ב ר א ה ל
ל ה ח ו נ ג ל ר ל י ו ל א ע ת ב ר ק ה ו ו ש ע ת א ל ה ד ב ע ה כ

○ SMALLPOX    ◇ IN 5765/2005    □ THE DEAD IN THE PLAGUE WERE 14,700

He looked at the code table where the year appeared, and saw that the plain text of the Bible crossing "smallpox" said, "The dead in the plague were 14,700."

"Those are the original words of the Torah," Kuperwasser said, surprised. "It's very close to our own estimates of a possible death toll."

"Both 'Jerusalem' and 'Tel Aviv' are also encoded with 'smallpox,' and so is 'in the End of Days,'" I told him, showing him the compter printouts.

ל ע ו י ס י ל כ ל כ ל ע ו ל ה ה א ל ע ה ה ז ה ו ר ו ה ט ש י א ס י
מ א י ו י ל ג י ר ש ל ה ש ה ז י י נ ⓗ י ה כ י ה י ד ל י ת י ש ע ה מ ס
ו פ י ל ע י ל ו ת ה ה ת ש פ מ ע ל ⓞ ת ה ס ת ה פ מ ש ל כ ר ש ש י ש י נ
ת ח נ י מ ו ו י ה י ת מ ם י ש ר ת ⓥ ה ע ב ר א ה ש י ס ב י ש ב
ת א ה נ ל ו ד י מ ה ש ר י ו ⓑ ה ע י ר צ מ ט ס ע ל ה ס ע י ה ש
ל ח נ ה י ש כ ב א ו ט י ע מ ת ⓥ ה מ ה ת נ א מ ו ב ר ת ה ר ה ת א
ש ר ר ע ת א ת ת נ ג ט ו ל י ⓑ ל י כ ה ש ה ת ו מ א ד ל ו
י ד ת ב ש ו [ס ו מ י ת ה י ר ח א ב] ה ל ה א נ ה י ס ה ד ת ל כ ל ד ו
ש ש י א ל ט א ר י ש ר י ע ס י ה ר ה ת ר י צ מ ל כ ו י ל ח
ל ה ש ע ר ש א ו י צ ק א ל כ ל ו ס ל צ מ ה ל ע ר פ ל

○ SMALLPOX    □ IN THE END OF DAYS

General Kuperwasser said he also took seriously the threat of an "atomic holocaust" in 2006. "It agrees with our own analysis of when one or more of our neighbors might attain nuclear capability," he said.

"The Americans are obsessed with Iraq," he commented. "We're more focused on Iran."

"Perhaps you should also take a look at Libya," I told him. "The Bible code very consistently suggests Libya will be the source of a weapon, even if the actual attack comes from terrorists."

Months later, on September 4, 2002, Prime Minister Sharon said on Israeli television, "Libya is becoming perhaps a more dangerous country than we thought. Libya may be the first Arab country with weapons of mass destruction."

I do not know if it was my warning to General Kuperwasser that finally made its way to the Prime Minister, but warnings from the Bible code I gave Israeli officials often later came out in the press attributed to intelligence reports.

I showed Kuperwasser the location of a possible terrorist base in Yemen or Iran. It was encoded by name in the Bible with every major danger to Israel—with "smallpox," with "atomic holocaust," and with "bin Laden."

But there were two locations with the same name, one in Yemen and one in Iran, both likely suspects in any hunt for terrorists.

"Isaac gave me the coordinates," said Kuperwasser. "We already looked. In Yemen, nothing. In Iran, we saw some activity, but nothing definitive. Maybe we looked too soon. Maybe we have to look in 2005 and 2006. We'll look again. We'll keep looking."

Kuperwasser clearly took the Bible code quite seriously. I asked him if he could help arrange for me to see Arafat, who was now isolated in his battered compound, surrounded by Israeli tanks.

"I met with Arafat a year ago," I told the general. "He believes in the Bible code, in fact I think he believes I'm a prophet. I told him that according to the code his only choice is peace or annihilation."

"He might believe you," said Kuperwasser, "but it doesn't mean Arafat sees it the same way you do. He might choose annihilation."

I knew Kuperwasser was no friend of Arafat. He had in fact just returned from Washington, on a mission from Sharon to persuade the White House that Arafat was a terrorist, and would never change.

In any event, Kuperwasser said there was nothing he could do to get me past the Israeli tanks to see Arafat. "Only the Prime Minister can approve it," he said.

---

On Holocaust Memorial Day I met in Jerusalem with Dan Meridor, the Israeli Cabinet Minister whose job it is to prepare for and prevent terrorist attacks with chemical, biological, and nuclear weapons.

I showed Meridor the two ultimate warnings in the Bible code. That Israel would be struck by a modern "plague"—"smallpox"—in 5765, the Hebrew year equivalent to 2005.

And then I showed Meridor the final warning, that Israel would face an "atomic holocaust" the next year, 2006.

"We already knew this was a probability," said Meridor. "And we already knew these years—2005, 2006—are the probabilities."

Meridor said it very matter-of-factly. He showed no emotion. He spoke like a bookkeeper who had just gone over the numbers, and confirmed that they added up.

It seemed to have no impact on him that we were talking about two terminal events, that we were sitting in the target, and that a 3000-year-old code in the Bible had gotten both years exactly right.

But it was a remarkable confirmation of the warnings in the Bible code from one of the few men in Israel who knew the numbers cold.

Both the CIA and Israeli intelligence had independently reached the same conclusion—that the threat of nuclear terrorism would peak between 2005 and 2007.

Israel's Defense Minister, Benjamin Ben-Eliezer, had just publicly stated that "around 2005 Iran will have nuclear capabilities that will threaten us, the region, and possibly the entire world."

And shortly after September 11, Meridor himself led a national security committee that warned Prime Minister Sharon that the most dangerous nonconventional threat Israel faced was smallpox.

Indeed, Meridor had just completed a lecture on the imminent threat of "nonconventional terrorism" at Israel's National Security College on September 11, when the first report of the attack on the Twin Towers came in.

"Unfortunately, this attack is only the beginning," he commented.

But although the warnings in the Bible code were virtually the same as the warnings in Israeli intelligence estimates, which the Cabinet Minister now confirmed, he said it as if to dismiss the prediction.

"We already knew this," he said again. "We don't need a code in the Bible."

"Perhaps," I replied, "but the code predicted these same dangers in these same years before your own intelligence services came to these same conclusions. And it appears in a text that's three thousand years old."

"I'm a rational person," said Meridor. "I don't believe in such things."

"It keeps coming true," I told Meridor.

"Shimon Peres will tell you that when I met with him right after Rabin was assassinated, in 1996, when Peres was Prime Minister, that I warned him of an 'atomic holocaust' in 2006," I said. "And, of course, I warned Rabin that he might be killed a year before the assassination."

I gave Meridor a copy of the letter I had sent Rabin. He read it, impatiently.

"Let's say I believe you," said Meridor. "What can we do?"

It was exactly what the Prime Minister's son Omri Sharon had said to me the last time we spoke. It was, more or less, what everyone said to me, whether they believed in the Bible code or not. And I did not have an answer.

"Take the years seriously," I said.

"I already do," said Meridor.

Beyond that, I had no real solution, except the warning I had already given Arafat, and was trying to give Sharon, the warning I had given Clinton, and was trying to give Bush—that the real choice was not peace or war, but peace or annihilation, and that no peace, even if made, would last until everyone understood that.

---

I had to see Sharon. In fact, I had made a note to myself before I left for Israel: "Sharon is the key. You must scare him as you scared Arafat." If there was to be peace, both of these old adversaries had to believe there was no choice but peace or annihilation.

Three top Israeli generals, Kuperwasser, Ben-Israel, and Dagan, all with a strong intelligence background, took the warnings in the Bible code seriously. The chief of intelligence analysis, the chief of scientific analysis, and the former chief of counterintelligence, the next chief of the Mossad, all believed the future might be foretold in a 3000-year-old code.

But I could not convince Israel's political leadership. I could not get to the one man whose decisions right now might decide the ultimate fate of Israel.

Prime Minister Ariel Sharon would not see me. His chief of staff quit on the day we were to meet, and there was no one else to turn to, no one I had not tried.

Before I left Israel I went back to see Eli Rips. We looked again at words we had found encoded in the Bible years earlier, right after the Rabin assassination—"Holocaust of Israel."

Now I pointed out to Rips that "Sharon" was encoded in the same place.

"Annexed" appeared twice on the same table. It was a clear warning that Israel's military victories, its occupation of Arab land, could lead to a new Holocaust.

I recalled the words of Israel's then Prime Minister Levi Eshkol, to the young Ariel Sharon, after the general's stunning victory in the 1967 war that helped Israel win the West Bank and Gaza.

O HOLOCAUST OF ISRAEL　　◇ SHARON　　□ ANNEXED　　□ ANNEXED

"Nothing will be settled by military victory," Eshkol told Sharon. "The Arabs will still be here."

But 35 years later, in June 2002, Sharon reinvaded the entire West Bank and once more made Arafat a prisoner in his own headquarters. And this time, Sharon said the Israeli occupation of Palestine might last years.

So in the summer of 2002, with Israeli tanks again occupying Palestine, the threat of a "Holocaust" encoded in the Bible appeared very real.

---

# CHAPTER TEN

# ALIEN

---

In our imagination, a spaceship lands on Earth and an alien emerges.

But scientists searching for intelligent life consider an alien landing the least likely form of contact. The huge distances required for interstellar travel—hundreds, or thousands, or millions of light years—make it almost impossible.

So SETI, the Search for Extraterrestrial Intelligence, has for ten years listened for radio signals from five hundred nearby sunlike stars. A giant array of satellite dishes, twenty-seven antennas in a Y pattern twenty-two miles wide, point up at the sky from an ancient lake bed in the New Mexico desert. So far, only silence.

As I prepared to launch my archaeological expedition in the Lisan—my search for the "code key," and for the "obelisks"—the National Aeronautics and Space Administration announced it will launch a new generation of unmanned spacecraft to search the cosmos for extraterrestrial life.

But even our galaxy, the Milky Way, has a hundred billion stars, and there are billions of galaxies.

There is, however, another alternative.

It's the contact scientists consider most likely—the discovery of an alien artifact on or near the Earth.

What if the long-awaited contact with another intelligence actually took place long ago? What if the Bible code is, in fact, the contact?

From the outset of my quest, I had known that there was something otherworldly about the Bible code. No human being could have looked 3000 years ahead and encoded the details of today's world into the Bible.

Indeed, the very existence of an ancient code key would suggest that thousands of years ago someone here on Earth had a science more advanced than we have today.

In his book *Are We Alone*? the Australian physicist Paul Davies imagines an artifact left behind by aliens —"programmed to manifest itself only when civilization on Earth crossed a certain threshold of advancement. Such a device—in effect, an extraterrestrial time capsule—could store vast amounts of important information for us."

That could be a perfect description of the code key.

The astronomer Carl Sagan noted that if there was other intelligent life in the universe, some of it would have evolved far earlier than we did, and would have had thousands, or hundreds of thousands, or millions, or hundreds of millions of years to develop the advanced technology that we are only now beginning to develop.

"What is for us technologically difficult or impossible," wrote Sagan, "what might seem to us like magic, might for them be trivially easy."

What if some magical code key really did exist? What if the obelisks were buried here on Earth by some unknown advanced civilization? What if they did indeed come from beyond this planet?

What if the most ancient commentary was right: "They were not what a human being had made, but the work of Heaven"?

It would be the first proof that we are not alone. I could not help but envision the moment we unearthed the monolith, obviously not of this world, but here on Earth. The big question man had been asking since the dawn of time would be answered: there was other life in the universe, and it had once been here.

But still I remained a skeptic. The more awesome the potential discovery, the less I could believe in it.

Even the fact that the Bible code consistently said that the obelisks, although thousands of years old, were preserved in a "steel ark," suggesting that they came from a more advanced civilization, did not fully convince me.

But when Nobel laureate Francis Crick confirmed what the code stated—that our "DNA was brought in a vehicle"—that the code of life was sent here in a "spaceship," I finally looked in the Bible code for the word I had so far avoided—"alien."

---

"Alien of Lisan" is encoded in the Book of Joshua, the only book in the Bible whose original words describe the exact location of our search.

Indeed, that verse of Joshua crosses "alien of Lisan." It pinpoints the finger of the peninsula that juts out into the Dead Sea, forming a small bay—"to the north of the bay at Lisan."

○ ALIEN OF LISAN  □ (TO THE NORTH) OF THE BAY AT LISAN, FROM THE EDGE OF THE JORDAN

"Alien of Lisan" is also encoded in the Torah, crossed in the plain text by the Biblical name for Jordan, "in a field of Moab, on the top of the hill."

○ ALIEN OF LISAN  □ IN A FIELD OF MOAB, ON THE TOP OF A HILL

It clearly stated a site in the Lisan, the cliff at the cape at the northern tip of the peninsula. Indeed, "cape" was encoded in the same place.

And just below that the original words of the Bible state, "He made for you a sculpture of all the forms that are in Heaven."

And there was much more in the code that appeared to confirm that the code key really did arrive here from another planet.

"Alien code" appeared in the Bible with "Mazra." "Detector" was in the same place. "Obelisk" and "key" were both encoded on the same table.

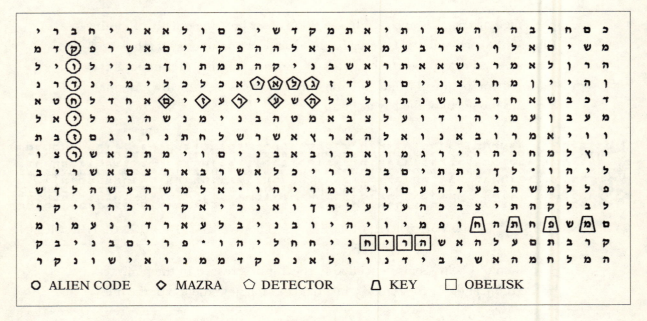

○ ALIEN CODE     ◇ MAZRA     ⬠ DETECTOR     △ KEY     ☐ OBELISK

"Code from alien" is encoded with "iron furnace," and "from Lisan" appears in the same place.

"Lisan alien," which in Hebrew also means "alien language," was also encoded crossed by "Mazra."

"Mazra" in Hebrew means "seeded area," and just above that "DNA" is encoded, suggesting again that the code of life as well as the Bible code are an "alien language."

O CODE FROM ALIEN     □ FROM IRON FURNACE     ◇ FROM LISAN

O LISAN ALIEN/ALIEN LANGUAGE     □ MAZRA/SEEDED

Was Crick right? Did both the genetic code and the Bible code arrive here in a "vehicle"?

I looked again at the code table where "steel vehicle" appeared with both "Mazra" and "Lisan." Now I saw that just above "steel vehicle" the hidden text stated, "forced down, intercepted."

In Hebrew, that word has only one meaning, the interception of an aircraft.

ל ש ה ל י א י ל ת פ נ ד ל מ י נ ד ע מ ו ת י א ו ה ו ו מ ח ל ה נ
צ מ ד ל מ ו ה י ל א ר ב ד ר ש א כ ו ש ע א ל ו ס י ה ל א ה ת א ת
ל ח ת ב ז צ ר א ל א י ס ו ב י ה ו י ו ח ה ו י ז ר פ ה ו י י מ ר א
ל ע ו מ ש ר ש א ל א ר ש י י נ ב **ש ט ר ו** ש ו כ י ו נ ב ת ה ת ו י ה
כ ה ש מ ל א י ו ה י ר מ א י ו י ה י ב ד ש א כ ס ה ל א ע מ
ר ש י ה נ ק מ ו י ב י ו ה י ה ל **פ** ה ו י ד א מ ד ב כ ר ב ד ן א צ ב
כ ה ה ר א נ כ ה י ה א ל י י ג פ **ל** ד א מ ד ב כ ס י ר צ מ ל ב ג ג
ה ל א ס ת ע ג ה ק ס ב ש א ס **ד** ב ס ת ל ב ט ו ב י ת א ה ד ג א
ע ו ס מ ו י י נ ע ה ד ו מ ע ש י **מ** י א ל ה ל י ל ו ס מ ו י ת כ ל
ה ש מ ע ס י י ס י מ ה מ ר ו ב ס כ **ו** ו ס ו ס ה א ג ה א ג י ב י ו ה
י נ פ ד מ ע י ב נ ת ה כ ב ל ה ו **ד** ד י ב ח ק ר א י ה ת א ב ב ת י
ה מ ר א ל ב י ב ס ס ע ת ה ת א ת ל **ג** ה ה ו י י ס ר ה ל ע ה ס ע ה ל
י ה י ו ו ס א ם א ו ס י ל ל פ ב ן ת נ ו ה נ ש א ה ל ע ב ו י ל ע ת
א ה נ ה ו מ א ב ל ח ב י ד ג ל ש ב ת א ל ד י י ל א י ו ה י ה י ב

○ STEEL, VEHICLE    □ FORCED DOWN, INTERCEPTED

This was surely science fiction. It could not be real. How could a space-craft have existed in ancient times? Obviously, only if it came from beyond.

"Alien on Earth" was encoded once in the Bible, remarkably again with "Mazra." And again, there was the suggestion that the arrival on Earth was not intentional: "by mistake, in error," crossed "alien on Earth."

The clearest sighting of a spaceship in the Bible is in the original words of the Book of Ezekiel. It is called the "Vision of the Chariot":

"And I saw, and behold, a tempest was coming from the north, a huge cloud and a flaming fire with a brightness around it; and from its midst it was like the color of the electric from the midst of the fire. And from its midst was the likeness of four living beings, and this is their appearance: they had the likeness of a man."

Encoded in the same place in Ezekiel are the words "human alien."

O ALIEN ON EARTH ◇ MAZRA □ BY MISTAKE, IN ERROR

O HUMAN ALIEN □ HUMAN NEARBY IN A CRYPT ◇ LISAN

"Lisan" appears with no skips in the same place, and overlapping it in reverse, the hidden text states: "Human nearby in a crypt."

There was another encoding in the Torah that seemed to confirm that a manlike creature came here long ago, and left us the Bible code.

"The alien is a man" appeared once in the Bible.

O THE ALIEN IS A MAN    □ LORD OF THE CODE    ◇ MOUTH OF THE OBELISKS

In the same place, in the original words of the Bible, appeared the two phrases that originally appeared with "code key"—"Mouth of the Obelisks" and "Lord of the Code."

It seemed quite clearly to suggest that the Encoder was a human, but not one of us. And again, in the same place, the code stated, "He was intercepted, forced down."

What, or who, could have intervened to force the crash landing of this ancient astronaut? There was no clue in the code.

But it all seemed an unmistakable statement that the code key arrived here on Earth in a spacecraft.

Was the "steel ark" an alien vessel?

The more compelling the evidence in the code became, the more I doubted it all.

I could believe that the key to the Bible code was engraved on an obelisk, and that the obelisk lay buried in a barren peninsula that had not been inhabited since before Biblical times. But I could not believe that it arrived here in a spaceship.

But Crick, who discovered the structure of DNA, said that our DNA arrived here in a spaceship sent by an alien. If the genetic code, why not also the Bible code?

The very existence of a code in the Bible that reveals the future proves that we are not alone. Since none of us can see across time, some alien intelligence must have once intervened in this world, at least at the time that the Bible was first written.

That, in fact, is the one shared belief of all religions. The Bible is on its face the story of a close encounter with an alien. He is not seen, but He is often heard.

In every ancient myth, in all religions, there are stories of vehicles and beings that descend from the sky, of fearsome visitors from other realms, of "boats of Heaven." Even God's descent on Mount Sinai is accompanied by smoke and fire.

But I don't believe in God. And although almost all scientists now agree that there is almost certainly other intelligent life in the universe, I won't really believe in little green men until they land here.

I'm a reporter. I want hard evidence.

---

On Shavuot, the holiday that celebrates the giving of the Bible by God to Moses on Mount Sinai, I found in the Bible code the final proof that the code key I was seeking was indeed on pillars encased in steel.

And in that same encoding, I found "God."

"In steel, obelisks" is encoded in the Bible crossed by a verse in Genesis that tells of the creation of mankind:

"In the image of God He made him, male and female He made them."

It was more than proof that the "obelisks" were indeed in some kind of "steel ark."

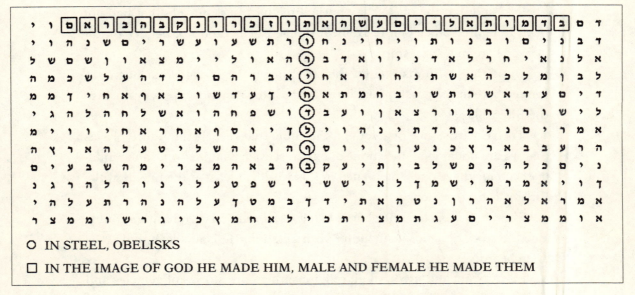

O IN STEEL, OBELISKS

□ IN THE IMAGE OF GOD HE MADE HIM, MALE AND FEMALE HE MADE THEM

The words of Genesis also seemed to confirm the only known ancient commentary about the "obelisks"—the statement in the Midrash that they were in human form, indeed that they were "male and female."

More than that, it seemed to link the obelisks to our creation, to our Creator:

"This is the book of the history of Man on the day that God created Man in the image of God."

The full passage in Genesis 5:1 that crossed "in steel, obelisks" seemed to confirm that the obelisks were the code key, that they would reveal our hidden past and our entire future.

The suggestion is that our future was known on the day of our creation, that the history of all mankind was written before it happened—so that if we were to read it now, we would see not only everything that had already happened, but everything that is yet to happen to the human race.

And the same code table reconfirmed the location of the "obelisks." "Pillar Lisan, tongue of sea" appears in exactly the same place.

○ IN STEEL, OBELISKS  □ PILLAR LISAN, TONGUE OF SEA

"In steel" we might find not only the "obelisks," but our true origins. The
full code matrix stated, "Lord, owner, will be recognized in steel, obelisks."

○ IN STEEL, OBELISKS  □  PILLAR LISAN, TONGUE OF SEA

◇  LORD, OWNER WILL BE RECOGNIZED IN STEEL, OBELISKS

It appeared to suggest that the obelisks are in the image of their creator, who may also be our Creator.

As I prepared to launch my search in the Lisan, I made a note in my journal: "I am forced to conclude that in addition to an 'obelisk' that is the 'code key,' I am also searching for the 'alien' who created it, or at least brought it here, and the 'vehicle' that he came in."

# CHAPTER ELEVEN

# B U S H

On August 3, 2001, I sent President George W. Bush a letter, telling him that "the Bible code warns that the world may face its ultimate danger—a nuclear World War, starting in the Middle East—while you are in office."

My letter reached his Chief of Staff, Andrew Card, at the White House just as Bush was leaving for a month-long vacation at his ranch in Crawford, Texas. Card sent it to the President's National Security Adviser, Condoleezza Rice. But my letter never reached the President.

On September 10, after Bush returned to Washington from his vacation, I called the White House to urge Card to give the President my letter, and arrange for me to see him.

"Mr. Card gave your letter to Dr. Rice," his chief assistant told me. "It was read by the two highest-ranking people here. But it is their decision not to give it to the President."

The next day, on September 11, 2001, Arab terrorists attacked New York and Washington, knocking down the World Trade Towers and damaging the Pentagon. The White House escaped attack only because the passengers of the fourth hijacked airplane forced it down before it could reach Washington.

The letter I sent Bush more than a month before 9/11 was not the only missed warning. Later, it was revealed that on August 6, at almost the same time my letter reached the White House, the CIA told the vacationing President that Osama bin Laden's followers in Al Qaeda might hijack commercial airliners. And an FBI report that never reached Bush warned that bin Laden might be sending operatives to flight schools in America to train for terrorist attacks.

Indeed, in mid-August one of them, now suspected to be the intended twentieth hijacker, was arrested. But the FBI failed to find the crucial clue that was on his laptop computer—a name that could have led to the leader of the 9/11 attack, Mohammed Atta.

And on September 10, 2001 the National Security Agency intercepted a message in Arabic: "Tomorrow is zero hour." But the critical communication was not translated until September 12.

I knew there was no point in the frenzied weeks after 9/11 to try to reach the President. But on October 1, I sent a new letter to Bush through both his Chief of Staff, Card, and his National Security Adviser, Rice.

I told them both the same thing: "If you just reread my letter in the light of September 11, I think you will now give it to the President. If he reads my letter, I think he will want to meet with me.

"You can tell the President that the attack on New York, that I saw happen with my own eyes, was encoded in the Bible 3000 years ago."

My October 1 letter to President Bush stated: "I'm not religious, so I can't explain how the future can be known, or why it is encoded in the Bible.

"But 'Twin Towers' is encoded with 'airplane,' and 'it will cause them to fall' appears in the same place. 'Pentagon' is encoded with 'damaged.' 'Bin Laden' is encoded with 'the city and the tower.'"

I told the President that the danger was not over: "The Bible code clearly states the final danger in modern terms—'atomic holocaust' and 'World War' are both encoded in the Bible. And both are encoded with the same year, 2006."

I closed my letter to Bush with an apology: "I'm sorry I did not warn you in advance of the terrorist attacks on New York and Washington. Both were encoded in the Bible 3000 years ago. But we didn't see it until September 11.

"If the Bible code is right, this was not the end of the danger, but the beginning. We can't see every danger in advance, but we can prevent those we do see.

"It may be important that we meet because it's likely the ultimate danger is real—we may really face a nuclear World War in five years."

---

"President Bush" is encoded in the Bible with "the second," and we found that months before the November 2000 election.

O PRESIDENT BUSH   □ THE SECOND

The 3000-year-old Bible code had accurately predicted the outcome of an election that was so close the votes were not counted and the victor was unknown until the Supreme Court declared Bush the winner more than a month later.

In fact, the entire cliff-hanger contest between Bush and his Democratic rival, Al Gore, was encoded. I had been following it in the Bible code before either candidate was even nominated.

Ten months before the closest election in American history, I went to see Dr. Rips in Nashville, Tennessee, where he was a visiting professor at Vanderbilt University. Rips told me he had given a lecture on the Bible code at a local synagogue, and in response to a question from the audience, he had looked in the code for a local hero, Clinton's Vice President, Al Gore.

Rips showed me the code table. "Al Gore" was encoded in Genesis with "President" against high odds.

○ AL GORE □ PRESIDENT

I told Rips that it seemed to me very unlikely that Gore would be President. Every poll had Bush way ahead. In fact, it was less than certain that Gore would even be the Democratic candidate.

So we looked for "President Bush," which was encoded with "President" crossing "President."

"This has no clear meaning," said Rips, "because you have already had a President Bush."

Then I showed Rips that "President Bush" was also encoded with "the second."

"What do you think this all means?" I asked Rips. "I don't know," he replied. "Perhaps that both Gore and Bush are probabilities, that both have a chance to be President."

Over the next ten months, Dr. Rips and I watched Bush and Gore get nominated, and then watched the once-lopsided race get closer and closer. Finally, the day after the election we spoke again.

It had been a wild night. First Gore called Bush to concede the election. Then Gore called Bush back to withdraw his concession. In the end, the outcome would be decided by a few hundred votes in one state, Florida.

"Now we know why the code had both Gore and Bush as probabilities," said Rips.

As the recounts and court battles dragged on for the next five weeks, I looked again in the Bible code for some clue to the final outcome. Now I saw that where "Al Gore" was encoded with "President Gore," the Hebrew

○ PRESIDENT GORE  ◇ AL GORE

☐ A JUDGE WILL RULE NOW, EVIL WILL BE DONE TO YOU

letters that followed his name clearly stated a very different outcome: "A judge will rule now, evil will be done to you."

Two hours before midnight on December 12, 2000, the United States Supreme Court stole the election from Al Gore, who had won the popular vote, by halting the Florida recount. George W. Bush, with the backing of all five conservative Republican justices, was declared the new President of the United States.

That night, I looked again at the Bible code table that had originally predicted a Bush victory. "By mistake, in error" appeared in the plain text just above "President Bush."

O PRESIDENT BUSH    □ PRESIDENT    ◇ BY MISTAKE, IN ERROR

But the most important encoding foretold the decisive moment in world history the new President would face.

"G. W. Bush" was encoded with "President" where the plain text of the Bible stated "in the End of Days."

ו ס י . ל א ח ו ר ו י י ל ע י ה ת ו ו י ט ב ש ל ו כ ש ל א ר ש י ת
י ע ו ל ג ו ל פ ב ה ז ת ם י י ר Ⓢ ה ז ח מ ר ש א ל א י ר מ א ע מ
ז י ם י ל ע ס ז ר א כ י . ו י י ע ט נ ס י ל ה א כ ר ה נ י י ז
י ו ב ג ל כ א י ו ל ס א ת פ ע ו ת כ ס י ר צ מ מ ו א י צ ו מ ל א
ף א י ה י ו י ו י א ד י י א ו י Ⓝ כ ב ד י כ ר ב מ ו מ נ י י ק י
ל ח ב ר ה ת נ ו ס י מ ע פ ש ל ש ה ז ר ב ר כ ת ב ר ב נ ה ו י ד י ת
ד י ל א ת ח ל ש ר ש א ד י א כ ל מ ל א ם ג א כ ל ה ק ל ב ל א ם ע ל
י ר ב ד י י ר ש א י ב ל מ ה ע ר ו א ה Ⓑ ו ט נ י ע ל י י ה י י ם
נ ז א י י ש מ א ש ⟨ד⟩⟨י⟩⟨ה⟩⟨ר⟩⟨ש⟩⟨י⟩⟨א⟩⟨צ⟩ ד מ ע ל ה ה ז ה
א ם י י י ע ל ל ג י ו ל ם נ ה ת י י ד ש ה ת ה מ מ ו י י ל ע ת ע
א ה י ה ו ת ש י ב ב ל כ ר ק ר ק ו ב א Ⓝ מ י א פ ח מ ו צ ל א ר
ל ש מ א ש י ו ל ק ל מ ע ר א ר ו י י נ א מ ד ר ש ד י ב א ה ה ל ב
ד נ פ ע ל ס ב י ו ד ב ל ו מ י ן ת י א ר מ א י י ו ל ש מ א ש י
ו י ר י ש א ו י ע י ו ס י ת כ ד י מ ס י צ Ⓝ ל א י ו מ ש מ ה י ר ה
ז ל ס ע ה ל ח י י ו ס י ט ש ב ל ⟦א⟧ ר ש י י ש י י ו כ ר ל ד ל ה
ר ח י ו ר י ע פ ל ע ב ל ש א ר ש ⟦י⟧ ד צ א ר ה י נ י ה י ל א ל י ת
מ י ה י י ף א ו י ו ח ב ש ו ⟦ש⟧ מ ש ה ד Ⓖ נ . י ה י ל ס ת א
א ל א ב ר ק י ו י א ב ל א ר י י ⟦נ⟧ ב מ ש י א ה נ ה ו ר י ע פ ל ע
א ו ב ר ז ע ל א ו ב נ ח ג י פ א ר י ד ע ל מ ה ה א ה פ ס י י כ

○ G. W. BUSH   □ PRESIDENT   ◇ IN THE END OF DAYS

---

I had known that the Bible code warned of bin Laden long before 9/11.
In the spring of 1998, when I visited Dr. Rips in Israel, he showed me a code
table that he believed revealed the true nature of God—"Judgment of God"
was intertwined with "Mercy of God."

"According to the Midrash," said Rips, "the world was created twice—it
was first conceived of from the point of view of absolute judgment, right
and wrong. Then God saw that the world could not exist this way, that there
was no room for human imperfection, and he added mercy.

"But it's not like mixing hot and cold water and getting lukewarm, it's
like mixing fire and snow and each preserves its separate existence. Those
may be the two strands in the Bible code."

As soon as Rips showed me the code table, however, I saw something else. "Bin Laden" appeared with no skips, perfectly spelled, crossing "Judgment of God."

ב ת ג ס ו י י ל א ר מ א ת ו ר ו ח ל נ ל ה ד ל ל י י ש ר א ה כ ל מ ן ב י
א י ה י ד ו ב ר מ א י י י ו ה י ל ו ח ת ש י ו ש י א ה ד ק י
ח א ת י ב י ו ה י י נ ח ד ר ד ב י ג א י י ד א ט ע מ ו מ א
א ו ב ל צ ר י י ו ן ב ל ו ש מ ו ח Ⓐ ה ק ב ר ל ל ה ל א ה ס י ר ב ד
ד ת א ו ע מ ש כ י ו ת ח א י ד י Ⓢ ע ס י ד מ צ ת ה א ו ז נ ה
י ע ה ל ע י מ ל ג ל ע ד מ ע Ⓗ נ ה ו ש י א ה ל א ב ב י י ש
א ב י ו ס י מ ל ג ל ס ו מ ק ו ת Ⓘ ב ה י ת י ס י נ א י צ ו ה
י ל ג ר ו ו י ל ג ר צ ח ר ל ס Ⓜ ו ס י ל מ ג ל א ו פ ס מ ו ב י ל
ר ב ד ר מ א י י ב ר ב ד י ת ר ב Ⓓ ס א ד ע ל כ א ר ל מ א י ו י
ו פ כ ו ד ב ק י ב נ א צ י ל ו ת Ⓛ י ל י ד ג י ת א מ י נ ד א ת א
י ו ה ת נ ק ז י י ח א י ⟦ ן ד א ל נ ב ⟧ י נ ד א ת ש א ת ר ה ש ד ת ל ו ת
כ נ א ר ש א י נ ג ע נ כ ה נ ת א ב ג י נ ב ל ה ש א ח ק ת א כ ל א מ ר כ
ל א י י ד א כ ל מ ר א ו י י ב ל ה ש א ת ח ק ל י י ה נ פ ש מ ל א
ל צ ה ו ד ו א כ ל מ א ל ש י י ו י פ ל י כ ב ל ת ת ר ש א י

O JUDGMENT OF GOD    □ BIN LADEN

I didn't say anything to Rips. I did not know how he would react. But I was shaken. To me it was as if, in a very Biblical sense, bin Laden was the chosen instrument of our destruction in the modern world, just as other enemies were a chosen instrument of God's wrath in Biblical times.

It was only after 9/11 that I showed Rips what I had found years earlier. His interpretation was very different. "It is a clear statement that God will judge bin Laden," said Rips. He told me that a friend in Israel had found another, similar encoding: "Cursed be bin Laden, and to the Messiah belongs vengeance."

I told Rips that I believed the job of dealing with bin Laden was up to us, to real people in the real world, whatever ultimate punishment bin Laden may face in a world to come.

But Rips remained focused on the religious perspective, which I realized was relevant because terrorism had become a religion, and bin Laden was its high priest.

Rips showed me something new he had found on the code table where the leader of the 9/11 attack was named. "Terrorist Atta" was crossed in the plain text of the Bible by "his soul was cut off before me, I am the Lord."

"That directly contradicts the belief of Atta and bin Laden that there will be an afterlife reward for their deeds," said Rips. "It is a clear Biblical statement of the exact opposite—it means that he will be punished in his afterlife."

Rips was dealing with the danger on the same level, in the same terms, as the terrorists. Both he and they saw it all primarily, even exclusively, in religious terms. After 9/11 the FBI found an extensive handwritten journal Atta had left behind, which made clear that he believed he was on a mission from God.

But for me, the Bible code was just information, an early warning system, and everything depended on how we used it to prevent the worst of the predicted dangers.

The first job was to find bin Laden.

As the United States launched its attack on bin Laden and his Taliban supporters in Afghanistan on October 7, 2001, and the CIA told Congress that there was a "one hundred percent" chance of another major terrorist attack, I looked in the Bible code for "bin Laden."

"Bin Laden," the code said, would become a fugitive, moving "from headquarters to headquarters."

"City of refuge" twice appears in the plain text of the Bible, in the same place. The original meaning of these verses is perhaps significant. They told of ancient "cities of refuge" where a "murderer" could escape retribution, and stated that the only way he could be killed was if he left a refuge. Perhaps that was how bin Laden would ultimately be caught.

○ BIN LADEN    □ FROM HEADQUARTERS TO HEADQUARTERS    ◇ CITY OF REFUGE

△ MURDERER    ⬭ CAPTURED

"Captured" was in fact encoded parallel to "bin Laden," suggesting that eventually he would be found.

Indeed, where "bin Laden" was encoded with "the next terrorist," the hidden text stated, "he moved, and he was killed."

But it appeared from the Bible code that bin Laden would not be killed or captured in Afghanistan. The code seemed to state that he would escape the American attack on his training camps and caves, and reestablish his terror network from a base elsewhere in the Middle East.

The Bible code named an exact place. It crossed both Hebrew spellings of "bin Laden," and clearly called the location his "army headquarters." The same location was clearly linked to every ultimate danger, including "atomic weapon," and "atomic holocaust," as well as "chemical attack" and "the next war."

The same desert location that had never appeared in any intelligence

O  BIN LADEN   ◇  THE NEXT TERRORIST

report was also encoded against very high odds with the two most likely tar-
gets—"New York" and "Jerusalem."

I gave the information to officials at a high level in both American and
Israeli military intelligence. I told them all that "it might be linked to bin
Laden, or the remnants of his group, Al Qaeda." I also told them that it
"might be the location of unconventional weapons, perhaps the source of
ultimate danger to Israel and the U.S."

I made it clear that there was no hard evidence to support what was
encoded in the Bible, and also that there was no clear time to look, that no

year was clearly encoded. Since the Bible code told the future, I did not know if this was the place bin Laden had already fled to, or where he and/or his terror network would later regroup.

"I don't know if the base is active now," I said. "But this may be the right time to find out, and it's certainly better to look too early than too late."

I told the Americans and the Israelis one other thing—each time the name of this terrorist base appeared in the Bible code, it was crossed by the words "Libyan weapon." It seemed to suggest that Libya would acquire some ultimate weapon that would be used by terrorists to attack the West.

Several months later, this news report was published in Israel: "Libya's efforts to attain nuclear weapons increasingly worry Israeli and American officials. The Libyan threat was discussed in a round of strategic talks between the two countries held last week in Washington."

The report in *Ha'aretz* stated, "Although Libya was not formerly included among countries in the 'axis of evil' cited by U.S. President George Bush earlier in the year, American officials consider it a 'threshold' state which is making efforts to develop weapons of mass destruction."

It was the same warning I had given Shimon Peres five years earlier, when he was Prime Minister of Israel—that "Libya" was encoded with "atomic holocaust," but that the real danger was nuclear terrorism.

A few days later, in a speech in Jerusalem, Peres publicly stated the warning, without mentioning the Bible code. The greatest danger facing the world, said Peres, was that nuclear weapons would "fall into the hands of irresponsible countries, and be carried on the shoulders of fanatics."

Now the code had given us the names of the fanatics, Osama bin Laden and his terrorist network Al Qaeda. And I hoped it would reveal exactly where they could be found.

---

In May 2001, as violence in the Middle East spun out of control, I sent a letter to Secretary of State Colin Powell at his home in Virginia.

I hesitated to contact Powell at home, but I wanted to catch him before he left on a diplomatic tour of Europe, amid rumors that he would also meet for the first time with Palestinian leader Yasir Arafat.

Israeli F-16 fighter jets had just struck the West Bank and Gaza for the first time since the 1967 Six Day War, in retaliation for a suicide bombing. Every instinct told me something terrible was about to happen, and that my best chance to reach Powell was now, at a moment of crisis, just after I had met with Arafat and Peres.

My May 19 letter to Powell stated: "I'm just back from the Middle East, where I met with Yasir Arafat and Shimon Peres. I hope to see Prime Minister Sharon.

"There may be a chance for a breakthrough, a new way to bring them together for peace talks. That's why I sent this letter to your home. I would normally go through official channels, but I saw in the *New York Times* today a report that you said 'if there was any solution I could come up with, any conference or meeting that could be held right away, I would leap at it.' There may be such a solution, at least a new opening.

"Arafat believes in prophecy. I spent more than an hour with him discussing predictions found in the Bible. At the end he seemed convinced that his only two alternatives are peace or annihilation.

"No one has tried to reach him on that level before, and it may be the key."

I told Powell about the hidden code in the Bible that appeared to reveal the future. I hoped it might reach him because I had seen in his autobiography that he was a religious man, that he had once taught Sunday school, that he believed in "the old-time religion."

So I told Powell what I had told Bush: "The Bible code warns that we may face a nuclear World War, starting in the Middle East.

"Even if you cannot believe there is a code in the Bible that predicts the future," I wrote Powell, "it may still be important that we meet, because Arafat clearly does.

"When Sharon also accepts that the real choice is peace or annihilation, then there may be peace," I continued. "But it doesn't matter if Sharon is

convinced by intelligence reports or by prophecy—as long as he under-
stands that what's at stake is survival."

In the end, Powell returned to the United States without seeing Arafat,
and he never responded to my letter. But within a month, Bush sent him
back to try to work out a cease-fire between Arafat and Sharon.

That failed effort was destined to continue for the next year and beyond,
but without success.

But in the Bible code there appeared to be some hope. "C. Powell" was
encoded with "chief of the summit," suggesting that the Secretary of State
might yet bring the two sides together.

But in the same place "Powell" was encoded, the danger was also clearly
stated, in the same words that crossed "G. W. Bush"—"in the End of Days."

○ C. POWELL   □ CHIEF OF THE SUMMIT   ◇ IN THE END OF DAYS

As the countdown to 2006 continued, I worried that I might not be able to reach the President, although he saw his war against terrorism as a religious crusade.

The Bible code seemed to warn that the war on terrorism Bush had declared, the war that had already been waged in Afghanistan, but now seemed to falter, with bin Laden still on the loose, might come to a terrible end.

"War of Bush" was encoded in the Bible with the ultimate warning— "the evil that will befall you in the End of Days."

○ WAR OF BUSH    □ THE EVIL THAT WILL BEFALL YOU IN THE END OF DAYS
◇ THE NATIONS UNDER ALL OF HEAVEN

The words in the plain text crossing "war of Bush" made clear that the danger was global: "The nations under all of Heaven."

"The next terrorist" was encoded with the danger everyone now feared most, "atomic."

○ THE NEXT TERRORIST   ◇ ATOMIC

"The next terror attack" was encoded with "bin Laden," and the only city in the world that was also encoded with both "atomic holocaust" and "World War"—"Jerusalem."

But the Bible code warned that the impact would be global. "World War" was encoded with "terrorism" and the Arabic word for "suicide bomber"—"Shahid"—appeared in exactly the same place.

I feared that the sum of all the warnings in the Bible code was this—

O  THE NEXT TERROR ATTACK    ◇ BIN LADEN    □ JERUSALEM

O  WORLD WAR    □ TERRORISM    ◇ SUICIDE BOMBER

that the world would be in a perpetual state of war for the next five years, not a conventional war, but an escalating series of attacks by terrorists using weapons of mass destruction, and counterattacks by the Western world.

It would be the war that no one wanted to admit, a war between us and militant Islam, a war between Western civilization and the religious fanatics who wanted to destroy it.

The battle had already been joined. Everything that I had been trying to warn of, everything I had seen encoded in the Bible, was about to become our reality. And I was not sure what to do.

---

All the warnings in the Bible code that had seemed so Apocalyptic when I first made them public five years earlier, even when I first contacted President Bush a month before 9/11, were now common wisdom, accepted reality, even an inevitability our leaders now feared they could not prevent.

All the top Bush Cabinet members and the President himself, said that a new terrorist attack, even an act of nuclear terrorism, was almost certain.

"The prospect of another attack against the United States is very, very real," said Vice President Dick Cheney. "Not a matter of if, but when."

Defense Secretary Donald Rumsfeld told a Senate committee that terrorists would obtain weapons of mass destruction: "They have chemical weapons, biological weapons, some shortly will have nuclear weapons.

"They inevitably are going to get their hands on them, and they would not hesitate one minute in using them," Rumsfeld said.

"We do face additional terrorist threats," he added. "The question is not if, but when, and where, and how."

"It's inevitable," said FBI Director Robert Mueller. "There will be another attack. We will not be able to stop it. I wish I could be more optimistic."

The problem had before always been to persuade world leaders that the ultimate dangers encoded in the Bible might be real. Now the problem was to persuade them that the ultimate dangers might be prevented if the warnings in the code were heeded.

# CHAPTER TWELVE

# HERO JOURNEY

On some mornings, as I woke up to the news of new terrorist threats, my search for the code key seemed like a dream.

In the face of bin Laden, with the memory of 9/11 still seared in my mind, with the terrible certainty that neither New York nor the world had seen the last of it, my desert adventure seemed irrelevant.

But I had an instinct that it was the solution, perhaps the only solution. We needed a miracle, an answer to a danger that existed on the scale of mythic horror.

Perhaps it required a mythic act: "A hero ventures forth from the world of common day into a region of supernatural wonder: fabulous forces are there encountered and a decisive victory is won: the hero comes back from this mysterious adventure with the power to bestow boons on his fellow man."

That is the classic "Hero Journey." The same adventure was told in all ancient cultures. It was so basic that Joseph Campbell entitled it *The Hero with a Thousand Faces.*

It is the story of Prometheus ascending to Heaven to steal fire from the gods, and bestow it upon man. It is the story of Jason setting sail to capture the Golden Fleece. It is in its most ancient form the story of Gilgamesh, the legendary Sumerian king who 6000 years ago fought his way to the sea that surrounds the world, dove to the bottom, and plucked the plant of immortality.

But inevitably, the otherworldly power so nobly won is lost when the hero reenters this world. It is stolen, it disintegrates, or it simply disappears.

And the moral of the story is always the same—that the real reward is not the great prize sought, but the journey itself. As Campbell put it, "The godly powers sought and dangerously won are revealed to have been within the heart of the hero all the time."

The journey, the adventure, was only his path to the discovery of what was already within.

Sometimes, as I searched for the "code key," for the "obelisks," for the magic talisman from another realm that would reveal our forgotten past and our entire future, I imagined that I was on my own Hero Journey.

But I was no hero. I was no mythological figure. If anything, I was an antihero, a cynical reporter who stumbled onto an ancient mystery in the modern world.

It may be, as Campbell says, that everything we need, the answers to all the ultimate mysteries, are already within each of us, that we just need to discover them within ourselves.

The Bible says very much the same thing. Moses, in his last words to the ancient Israelites before he died, said it plainly: "It is not hidden from you, neither is it far off. It is not in Heaven, that thou shouldst say, Who shall go up for us to Heaven, and bring it to us that we may hear it, and do it? Nor is it beyond the sea, that thou shouldst say, Who shall go over the sea for us, and bring it to us that we may hear it and do it? But the word is very near to thee, in thy mouth, and in thy heart, that thou mayest do it."

Maybe. Maybe the journey, the quest, was just a way of unlocking the secret that lies inside. But as I read it, these famous words from the Bible offer real hope that we will one day find the "code key," unearth the "obelisks," because they are here on Earth, close at hand, within reach.

In the Bible, where Moses speaks his final words—"It is not in Heaven, that thou shouldst say, Who shall go up for us to Heaven?"—"in Lisan" is encoded with "Mazra."

⬡ IN LISAN   ◇ MAZRA   ☐ WHO SHALL GO UP FOR US TO HEAVEN?

This was not some metaphysical statement that the quest is just a way of unlocking the secrets that lie inside. It is a direct statement that a physical object lies buried in this exact spot.

However improbable it seemed that I would find the treasure, I always believed that the Bible code meant exactly what it said. "Lisan" and "Mazra" were real geographical locations, the ✕ on the treasure map.

Dr. Rips agreed that "Lisan" and "Mazra" could not appear consistently by chance, that it could not be an accident that "obelisks" twice crossed "code key." But as always, he would not guess what meaning that had in the real world.

"Nothing would be more exciting than finding material remnants, ancient objects, led there only by the Bible code," said Rips. "But I can only observe the consistency, I can only say that mathematically it is far beyond chance. I cannot say it means that the obelisks actually exist."

But no matter how unlikely it seemed that a flat-footed reporter would stumble onto some ultimate secret, I believed that something extraordinary—not of this world, yet in this world—would be found buried beneath that barren peninsula.

It might even halt the countdown to Armageddon.

———————————————————

The evidence in the Bible code seems clear, beyond doubt. It is stated by the best-known fortune-teller in the Bible, Joseph. His words are definite: "This is the solution."

It confirms that in some long forgotten time, something magical came down to Earth, in exactly the place where I'm looking, and it remains there for us to find today.

Hidden in Joseph's story is absolute confirmation of the existence of the code key, and its secret location.

Sold into slavery by his jealous brothers, Joseph rose to become the virtual ruler of Egypt by telling the pharaoh the future. He predicted a famine that saved all of Egypt from starvation. The pharaoh made Joseph his regent, put a gold chain around his neck, and gave Joseph a new name: "Zaphenath-Paneah."

For thousands of years, great sages have debated its meaning. Some believe it is a Hebrew translation of Egyptian hieroglyphics, and means "revealer of secrets." Others say the original pictographs of birds and snakes mean "the God speaks and lives."

But, in fact, the name has a very clear meaning in Hebrew—"Decoder of the Code."

So the existence of the Bible code, the code that tells the future, is actually revealed in the original words of the Bible.

And encoded across "Decoder of the Code," I now saw the very object of my search—"Key." It appeared with "steel on cape."

○ DECODER OF THE CODE  □ KEY  ◇ STEEL ON CAPE

"This is the solution," says Joseph when he twice reveals the future. And both times, right there, the location of the code key is revealed—"Lisan."

"This is the solution." It is as if the ancient prophet was revealing in the most direct possible way exactly where to look for the "key" that would "decode the code"—on the peninsula that jutted out into the Dead Sea, "Lisan."

"Code of God" is encoded where "Lisan" crosses "this is the solution."

It could not be more clear. Another code matrix stated "he found the exact place, Mazra," and that also appeared with "Lisan," and with "this is the solution."

○ CODE OF GOD     ◇ LISAN     □ THIS IS THE SOLUTION

○ HE FOUND THE EXACT PLACE, MAZRA     ◇ LISAN     □ THIS IS THE SOLUTION

    In the story of the ancient fortune-teller, I had found hidden confirmation of every essential detail of my quest.

    "Steel ark," "iron ark," "DNA on obelisk," "Creation of Man," and "Code of God" are all encoded with Joseph's words: "This is the solution," and the name of the location, "Lisan."

The "key" that is the "decoder of the code" would be found in some metal vessel, and would reveal to us both the Bible code and the code of life.

---

The proof is not just in the Torah, but also in the later books of the Bible.

"Code key" is encoded in Job, with a hidden text that states "in the lash-like appendage of Lisan."

O CODE KEY ◇ IN THE LASH-LIKE APPENDAGE OF LISAN

Again, it is an absolutely precise statement of the location, the finger of land that juts out into the Dead Sea from the northern end of the peninsula, forming the Bay of Mazra.

"He found the exact place, Lisan" is encoded in Joshua, where a verse in the plain text describes the same location: "Lisan, tongue of sea, to the edge."

⚪ HE FOUND THE EXACT PLACE, LISAN ◇ LISAN, TONGUE OF SEA, FROM THE EDGE

There is a treasure map encoded in the Bible. It confirms that we are looking in the right place. It states that the object still exists today.

If we can find the code key, if we can find the obelisks, then we might even find the identity of the Encoder.

---

Who is the Encoder?

The scientist who discovered the code, Dr. Rips, already had his answer. The code, like the Bible itself, came from God.

"It comes from an intelligence that is not merely higher, but different," said Rips. "It sees across time, it exists across time. Everything we think and do was anticipated."

But I do not assume that the Encoder is the Creator. For me, the existence of the code does not prove the existence of God—it just proves the existence of the Encoder.

There is a persistent suggestion in the code that the Encoder is in some way still alive. Indeed, the very word "Encoder" in Hebrew also means "he is encoding."

I asked Dr. Rips if the Bible code might be an ongoing dialogue with mankind. Was it possible that the Bible was being encoded in real time—that we were getting answers to our questions at the moment we asked them, not from an intelligence that existed long ago, but right now?

"I can imagine an intelligence that exists across time, for whom the past and the present and the future are one," said Rips. "So that even though you are asking the questions 'now,' and the Bible was encoded in the distant 'past,' from the point of view of the Encoder, it's all happening at once—including the 'future' he is revealing through the code."

It is not only Rips, a religious man who believes in an eternal God, who can imagine such an anomaly. It is also what Einstein said: "The distinction between past, present and future is only an illusion, however persistent."

But to me it was still not the full answer. I didn't want a metaphysical concept. I wanted hard evidence.

Did the Bible code come from a man, a god, or an alien?

The plain text of the Bible gives us only one clue. The original words very clearly say that God came down on Mount Sinai and gave Moses the Bible.

"Codes of Moses" appears in the hidden text with "Encoder" against the highest odds.

O CODES OF MOSES ◇ ENCODER

ies, would involve distances so great that it would require that we move faster than light. To do that, we would have to warp space-time.

According to most physicists, that would automatically mean that we would travel in time as well as space, specifically that we would go back in time.

Did some ancient astronaut come to Earth long ago, not merely from another place, but from another time?

---

My real quest was always to identify the Encoder.

Once I knew there was a code in the Bible that told the future, I had to know who it came from.

The existence of the Bible code is the first scientific evidence we've ever had that we are not alone, since no man can see across time.

The Encoder remains unidentified. But he may be leading us to him, a step at a time.

Maybe my search for the code key was only a journey that revealed to me levels of reality I never otherwise would have recognized, caused me to ask the cosmic questions raised by the very existence of the Bible code, and perhaps even led me to stumble upon the origin of life.

But I remain certain I will find the code key, the obelisks, perhaps even see the face of the Encoder.

"I have no doubt that behind all the code tables you are finding, there is some reality," said Rips. "But I cannot say if it is a physical reality, or a metaphysical reality."

It was the question I had long been asking myself. Did the code key belong to this world, or to some other realm?

"If it's metaphysical, it's more real, closer to the ultimate source of all reality," said Rips. "But maybe what you were seeking can only be seen with spiritual tools, because it requires contact with another realm."

I asked Rips why the Bible code would consistently, intentionally, present false information, lead me to a location where nothing exists.

"It's not false, it just exists on another level," said Rips. His advice was practical. He agreed with my basic instinct that "Lisan" meant Lisan, "Mazra" meant Mazra, that the "obelisk" was a physical object, on which was encoded the "key."

"A magnetometer, low frequency radar, the technology that does exist, this is obviously the first thing to try," said Rips. "But you may be standing in exactly the right place, and still not see it, because the tools we now have cannot see the object beneath your feet."

The real question might be not if the Bible code is right or even if we had interpreted it correctly, but whether our technology is advanced enough to find what is there. The code key may be as beyond our reach now as the Bible code itself was to those who received it 3000 years ago. It may require a technology not yet invented, a science not yet known.

We will not know the answer unless we are allowed to dig up what now may lie buried in the Lisan.

Will we find there the first evidence that we're not alone? Will that revelation end the mindless cycle of violence in the Middle East? Or will the warfare prevent us from ever finding the code key?

Will we find it in time to receive the warning we need to survive?

---

Who cared enough about us to reach across time to try to save us from some foreseen disaster?

It is no accident that some intelligence able to see the future created a code designed to be found at this one moment in human history. It had a time lock. It could not be found until the computer was invented.

There can be only one reason—we need the information now.

"Atomic attack" is encoded in the Bible, with the location of the code key, "Lisan," and "this is the solution."

"Atomic attack" is also encoded with 2006, the same year that appears with "atomic holocaust," "World War," and the "End of Days."

If the Bible code is right, we are facing the ultimate horror, not some

○ ECONOMIC CRISIS　◇ FROM 5762/2002　◇ 5690/1929　□ THE DEPRESSIONS

□ STOCKS

week that saw the worst stock market crash since 1929, since the Great Depression.

Two months later, the government made it official. We were in a "recession." The *New York Times* reported it: "The struggling U.S. economy slipped into a recession, snapping a record 10-year-long expansion." In fact, the *Times* stated, the entire world was suffering its first recession in two decades.

For a while it looked like the world might climb back out. But by the summer of 2002, the worst bear market in a generation sent all the major stock indexes back down below the depths they hit right after 9/11.

The Dow fell far below 8000, losing 1500 points in the ten days following the President's visit to Wall Street, the Standard & Poor's index fell below 800 for the first time in five years, the Nasdaq lost 75 percent of its value, and the whole market lost more than $7 trillion in just two years.

The stock market ended the Hebrew year 5762 on Friday, September 6, 2002, with losses on six of the last eight trading days, and in each of the last five months.

It was the first time the Dow had been down five months in a row since the 1981 recession. The *Times* reported that "it now looks likely to fall for three consecutive years, the longest stretch since the Depression."

The first Bible code prediction had already been fulfilled. An "economic crisis" had "started" in the Hebrew year 5762. The only question was how deep the "economic crisis" might become, whether the "recession" of 2002 would become a real "depression" in the years that followed.

My fear was not that we would face hard times. We could get through that. We had before. My fear was that the next two Bible code predictions would also come true.

My fear was that if the code predicted an "economic crisis" starting in 2002 four years in advance, it might also be right that we faced the "End of Days" in 2006.

In any event, it had been obvious since September 11 that the world was in unprecedented danger.

"New York," "Jerusalem," and "Tel Aviv" are all encoded with "small-pox."

The United States has ordered a half million health-care workers, the frontline in any bioterrorist attack, to be vaccinated. Israel has stockpiled enough smallpox vaccine for its entire population.

Israel first focused on the threat of smallpox as a weapon at the time of the Gulf War, more than ten years ago. But according to its chief military scientist, General Isaac Ben-Israel, everyone concluded that even Saddam Hussein would not be so crazy as to unleash smallpox. If Israel were attacked, it would be the same as attacking the Palestinians, Jordan, Lebanon, Syria, Egypt, finally the entire Middle East including Iraq.

"So we concluded there was no immediate danger," said Ben-Israel. "But now there's Osama bin Laden."

One "suicide carrier" boarding an airplane in Karachi or Kabul could fly to New York or Tel Aviv and begin a plague that could kill one-third of the world's population.

---

It was obvious that we had reached a critical moment in human history when the weapons we had built had escaped our control and would soon be, if they were not already, in the hands of rogue states and random lunatics.

It was why the "End of Days" looked so real to me right now. It was what I had been warning world leaders for years.

"If the Bible code is right, nuclear terrorists may trigger the next World War," I wrote five years ago in my first book of code predictions. "Instead of a nuclear war between superpowers, the world may now face a new threat— terrorists armed with nuclear weapons.

"World War II ended with an atomic bomb. World War III may start that way."

The warning signs had been around, even glaringly obvious, for more than ten years, ever since the collapse of the Soviet Union. As a Senate report at the time noted, "Never before has an empire disintegrated while in possession of 30,000 nuclear weapons."

Calling the former Soviet Union a "vast potential supermarket of chemical, biological and nuclear weapons," the Senate report warned that "the probability that one, two, or a dozen weapons of mass destruction detonating in Russia, or Europe, or the Middle East, or even the United States, has increased."

Weapons that were once available only to a handful of superpowers were suddenly on the black market, available to anyone who could pay the price, and we had done almost nothing to prevent the fire sale.

In fact, in one of his first acts after taking office, President Bush cut $100 million from the program Clinton had created to buy up Russian weapons and nuclear material, and Congress refused to approve payments to unemployed Soviet military scientists.

Now unstable third-world countries like Pakistan have nuclear weapons, which could fall into the hands of Islamic extremists tomorrow, and soon rogue nations like Iraq, Iran, and Libya will either buy or make their own nuclear arsenals.

It is known that bin Laden tried to acquire nuclear weapons, and it is possible that Al Qaeda succeeded in building a "dirty bomb," not a nuclear weapon, but a conventional bomb laced with radioactive material that could make any major city uninhabitable.

Until recently, we pretended that the nightmare could never really happen. In the words of a *New York Times* report, "The best reason for thinking that a nuclear terrorist attack won't happen is that it hasn't happened yet, and that is terrible logic."

As the chilling headline in the May 2002 *Times* story by senior editor Bill Keller stated, "SOONER OR LATER, AN ATTACK WILL HAPPEN HERE."

It was a watershed moment in American journalism, although the story appeared ten years too late, ten years after the danger should have been fully apparent. But in the post-9/11 world, the *Times*, the newspaper of record, finally stated the obvious: "All September 11 did was turn a theoretical possibility into a felt danger."

It gave one example, a computer model of what would happen if a 1-kiloton nuclear device was exploded in Times Square. Not a 500-kiloton warhead, but a nuclear land mine that could be carried on the back of one man.

One man with a weapon in a backpack could destroy the center of any city. If it happened in New York, this would be the horror:

Twenty thousand people would die in a matter of seconds. For more than a quarter mile beyond ground zero, anyone exposed to the fireball would die a gruesome death within a day. A quarter million people live in that radius. A mushroom cloud would go up more than two miles into the air, and then lethal fallout would begin drifting back to Earth, spreading up to ten miles.

If instead a 1-megaton bomb were dropped on New York, it would flatten every building in Manhattan. According to Jonathan Schell, in his definitive book *The Fate of the Earth*: "The physical collapse of the city would certainly kill millions of people. At a distance of 2 miles from ground zero, winds would reach 400 miles an hour. The fireball would grow until it was more than a mile wide, and rocket upward, to a height of over six miles. For ten seconds, it would broil the city below. Soon, huge thick clouds of dust and smoke would envelop the scene, and as the mushroom cloud rushed overhead (it would have a diameter of about 12 miles), the light of the sun would be blotted out and day would turn into night."

It is considered more likely that if New York were struck, it would be with a 20-megaton bomb: "The fireball would be about four and half miles in diameter. People caught in the open twenty-three miles away from ground zero would be burned to death. New York City and its suburbs would be transformed into a flattened scorched desert in a few seconds."

But most likely, nuclear terrorists would set off a bomb on the ground. Again, from Jonathan Schell: "If a 20-megaton bomb were ground-burst the fireball would be almost six miles in diameter, and everyone within it would be instantly killed, with most of them physically disappearing. New York City and its population, now radioactive dust, would rise into a mushroom cloud."

I fear that one morning we will wake up to the news that a whole city has been destroyed—not two big buildings, but an entire city—that New York, or Tel Aviv, or Jerusalem just does not exist any more.

---

September 11 would suddenly become a distant memory. The event that changed the world would be forgotten when the world changed again.

We are already living in that new world, in denial, yet waiting for it to happen.

"President Bush says that the September 11 attack on the United States marks a new kind of war," terrorism expert Robert Wright wrote in the *Times* two weeks after 9/11. "There is a sense in which that's true, but what's chilling is the sense in which it's not. The terrorists did not use biological or nuclear weapons, and next time they well could. A future enemy assault could kill not 6,000 people on American soil, but 600,000."

The warning in the Bible code, the ultimate warning of the "End of Days," was not encoded to prepare us for 9/11. The events of 9/11 may have happened to prepare us for the "End of Days."

The more closely we looked at the warnings in the Bible code, the clearer it became that the ultimate danger centered on 2006. That is the year most clearly encoded with "Atomic Holocaust" and "World War," and also with the "End of Days."

If the countdown began on September 11, 2001 then we have five years and counting from that date to find a way to survive.

Look again at what is encoded in the Bible: "Atomic Holocaust" with "in 5766," the year 2006.

○ ATOMIC HOLOCAUST     □ IN 5766/2006

"World War" is also encoded with "in 5766," again 2006.

○ WORLD WAR     □ IN 5766/2006

Listen again to what the scientist who discovered the Bible code, Dr. Rips, stated about the mathematical odds of "Atomic Holocaust," and "World War" and the "End of Days" all appearing with the same year, 2006—"the odds against it happening by chance are at least 100,000 to 1."

☐ IN THE END OF DAYS   ○  IN 5766/2006

And yet Rips offered hope. He noted that where the Hebrew year "in 5766" was encoded with "in the End of Days," it was where Moses warned of "the evil that will befall you in the End of Days."

He opened the Bible, and read the extended passage in Deuteronomy, where Moses spoke his last words before his death, and laid out two alternatives, the path of evil, and the path of righteousness.

"It's not a prediction," said Rips, "but a warning of what can happen, according to what we do."

Without making any Biblical references, that was exactly what I had told every world leader. The Bible code, I always said, stated probabilities, not determined events. What we did determined what actually happened.

The Bible code is not a prediction that we will all die in 2006. It is a warning that we <u>might</u> all die in 2006, if we do not change our future.

What we do here and now, here on Earth, will determine our fate.

# CODA

The greatest scientist who ever lived, the man who single-handedly invented modern science, Sir Isaac Newton, was certain that not only the Bible, but the entire universe, was a "cryptogram set by the Almighty," a puzzle that God made, and that we were meant to solve.

Since Newton, more than anyone before or since, did solve the puzzle, perhaps he was right.

Modern science was not enough. Newton realized we also needed ancient wisdom to solve the ultimate mysteries. Before he died three hundred years ago, Newton locked away thousands of handwritten papers. When the great economist John Maynard Keynes discovered them at Cambridge, he expected to find Newton's notes on gravity and calculus. Instead he found a million words about civilizations long gone, the Bible code, and the Apocalypse.

"Newton was not the first of the age of reason," wrote Keynes. "He was the last of the magicians, the last of the Babylonians and Sumerians, the last great mind that looked out on the visible and intellectual world with the same eyes that began to build our intellectual inheritance."

Newton would have wanted to see the words engraved on the obelisks.

In a simpler, more secular way, it's also always been my faith as a reporter—all puzzles can be solved.

It seemed to me no accident that as we were cracking the Bible code, scientists were simultaneously cracking the genetic code, that mankind was discovering its own DNA blueprint just at the moment that we were also perhaps deciphering a revelation in the Bible of our true origins and ultimate future.

Also, at the same time, the Hubble Space Telescope was sending back to Earth images that came ever closer to capturing light from the beginnings of the universe, from the moment of the theorized "Big Bang." And some scientists now believed that imprinted at the moment of Creation were a few mathematical statements, perhaps just six numbers that determined the shape of everything.

As the British astronomer Sir Martin Rees stated, these few numbers might explain "how a single 'genesis event' created billions of galaxies, black holes, stars and planets, and how atoms have been assembled—here on Earth, and perhaps on other worlds—into living beings intricate enough to ponder their origins."

In some way, it has all been made accessible to us. After just 6000 years of human civilization, we are closing in on the answers to ultimate mysteries. But with the answers perhaps almost within our grasp, we might, if the Bible code is right, be facing annihilation.

It is as if some force of good wants to reveal everything to us, and some force of evil wants to destroy us before we can achieve our destiny.

In any event, it seems that the object we need, both to survive, and to gain the final insight, is the "code key" buried in Lisan.

# CHAPTER NOTES

Dr. Rips used the standard Hebrew language text, known as the *Textus Receptus*, in his Bible code computer program, which is the basis for the code research cited in this book. The software I used was developed by Rips and his computer programmer Dr. Rotenberg.

All Torahs—the first five books of the Bible in Hebrew—that now exist are the same letter for letter, and cannot be used if even one letter is wrong.

The best-known edition of that text, *The Jerusalem Bible* (Koren Publishing Co., 1992), contains the most widely accepted English translation of the Old Testament, and is the primary source of quotes from the plain text in this book.

I have also consulted and sometimes used a translation some scholars prefer by Rabbi Aryeh Kaplan, *The Living Torah* (Maznaim, 1981).

Quotes from the New Testament are primarily from the King James Version, although I have also consulted a modern translation known as the New International Version.

The statements by Rips quoted throughout this book come from a series of conversations I had with him over the course of five years, primarily at his home in Jerusalem and in his office at Hebrew University, and in hundreds of telephone interviews.

Many of the events described in the book were witnessed by me. Accounts of other events are based on interviews with persons directly involved or were confirmed by published news reports.

The names and events encoded in the Bible use the same Hebrew that appears in the plain text of the Bible, and the same Hebrew used by Israelis today. The names of people and places are taken from standard reference sources like the *Hebrew Encyclopedia*. The Hebrew spellings for more current events are those used by Israeli newspapers.

The translations of all encodings have been confirmed by the authoritative R. Alcalay Hebrew-English dictionary (Massada, 1990) and the standard unabridged Hebrew dictionary, A. Even-Shoshan (Kiryat-Sefer Press, 1985).

The years encoded in the Bible are from the ancient Hebrew calendar, which starts in Biblical times, 3760 years earlier than the modern calendar. The current year, 2002, is roughly equivalent to the Hebrew year 5762. But Hebrew years begin in September or October, according to the lunar calendar, and end in September or October of the following year.

All of the Bible code printouts displayed in this book have been proven by statistics to be encoded beyond chance. The statistics are calculated automatically by the Rips-Rotenberg computer program. The computer scores the matches between words using two tests—how closely they appear together and whether the skips that spell out the search words are the shortest in the Bible.

Each code word determines how the computer presents the text of the Bible, what crossword puzzle is formed. The original order of the letters is never changed.

We can use our search for the "End of Days" as a case study. The words from Daniel are encoded with a skip of 7551. So the computer divided the entire original Bible—the whole strand of 304,805 letters— into 40 rows of 7551 letters. The Bible code printout (p. 16) shows only the center of that code table.

If the "End of Days" was spelled out with a skip of 100, then the rows would be 100 letters long. If the skip was 1000, then the rows would be 1000 letters long. And, in any event, the rows are stacked one on top of another, never changing the original order.

Three thousand years ago the Bible was encoded so that the words of Daniel that predict the "End of Days" would appear exactly where the words of Moses predicted what would happen "in the End of Days." And, 3000 years ago, it was also encoded so that the names of current world leaders would appear in the same place.

The opening quote by Nobel laureate physicist Richard Feynman comes from a lecture he gave at the University of Washington in April 1963, published in *The Meaning of It All* (Helix/Addison-Wesley, 1998). Feynman, who many consider the most important physicist since Einstein, also stated, "The only thing that can be predicted is the probability of different events" (*Six Easy Pieces*, Helix, 1995, p. 135).

The ancient commentary on the Bible called the Talmud states something similar: "Everything is foreseen, but freedom of action is given." For almost 2000 years sages have debated the apparent paradox—how can there be human free will if God knows everything in advance? The Bible code poses the same question, even for the secular. The answer appears to be what science states—that there are only probabilities, that there isn't just one future, but many possible futures. We determine the outcome.

## CHAPTER ONE: END OF DAYS

The events of September 11, 2001 were witnessed by me, and the details were confirmed by news reports in *The New York Times*, *Time* and *Newsweek*. I did not see any immediate television coverage, because all the broadcasts I received came from the World Trade Towers.

Dr. Rips sent me by e-mail the same Bible code table I found minutes after the towers fell, but the telephone lines were blocked, and it did not reach me until the next day. What was most striking to him, as a mathematician, was that the three words anyone would automatically look for,

"Twin" and "Towers" and "airplane," were encoded together in the same place against odds of 10,000 to 1. In Israel, the Word Trade Center was known as the "Twin Towers."

John Podesta, Chief of Staff at the White House, told me that President Clinton had my book with him at Camp David, when he met there in July 2000 with Arafat and Barak.

My meeting with Arafat in Ramallah took place April 13, 2001. My meeting with Shimon Peres at the Foreign Ministry in Tel Aviv took place April 22, 2001. My meeting with Omri Sharon was on April 17, 2001, at the King David Hotel in Jerusalem. I met with Podesta in the White House October 16, 2000.

My letter to President Bush was dated August 3, 2001, and I called the White House September 10, 2001. I was told that his Chief of Staff, Andrew Card, and his National Security Advisor, Condoleezza Rice, both received it.

The President's statement that "the first war of the 21$^{st}$ century has begun" was quoted in *The New York Times*. The *Times* column by Thomas Friedman headlined "WORLD WAR III" appeared September 13, 2001.

Sir Isaac Newton's search for a code in the Bible was described in the essay "Newton, the Man" by the famous economist John Maynard Keynes (*Essays and Sketches in Biography*, Meridian Books, 1956). Richard S. Westfall, in *The Life of Isaac Newton* (Cambridge University Press, 1993, p. 125), also quoted Newton's notebooks, and stated that the physicist "believed that the essence of the Bible was the prophecy of human history."

In Rips's statement that Newton could not find the code because it was "sealed until the time of the End," he is quoting from the Book of Daniel 12:4.

The legendary original form of the Bible dictated to Moses by God—"contiguous, without break of words"—was stated by the thirteenth-century sage Nachmanides in his *Commentary on the Torah* (Shilo, 1971, Charles Chavel, ed., Vol. I, p. 14). The continuity of the Bible is also expressed in its traditional form as a scroll, one continuous parchment that is unrolled.

The original Bible consists of the first five books, Genesis through Deuteronomy. Jews call it the Torah. But in this book I refer to it as the Bible, and to the code in it as the Bible code.

Rips's original experiment was published in *Statistical Science* in August 1994 (Vol. 9, no. 3), pp. 429–38, "Equidistant Letter Sequences in the Book of Genesis," Doron Witztum, Eliyahu Rips and Yoav Rosenberg. It reported that the names of 32 rabbis who lived after Biblical times matched the dates of their birth and death in the Bible code against odds of 4 in a million. In a series of later experiments the actual odds were found to be 1 in 10 million.

The U.S. National Security Agency code-breaker Harold Gans told me the results of his independent experiment in two telephone interviews, January 1993 and December 1996.

Gans stated the odds of also finding the names of the cities encoded with the names of the rabbis were 1 in 200,000.

I first heard about the Bible code by chance in June 1992, after meeting with General Uri Saguy, who was then Chief of Israeli Military Intelligence.

I first met with Dr. Rips at his home in Jerusalem in late June 1992. The Gulf War encoding he showed me that night was originally found by his colleague Witztum. Rips confirmed that Witztum told him the date of the first Scud missile attack on Israel, and that Rips himself saw it encoded in the Bible, three weeks before the Gulf War started.

Chaim Guri met with me at his home in Jerusalem September 1, 1994. He called Rabin's office that night, and the next morning the Prime Minister's driver picked up my letter warning of the encoded assassination, and delivered it to Rabin. The letter was dated September 1, 1994.

Rabin was murdered at a political rally in Tel Aviv on the evening of November 4, 1995. Yigal Amir, a 26-year-old Orthodox Jew, fired three shots, hitting Rabin twice in the back.

The four mentions of the "End of Days" in the Torah appear in Genesis 49:1, Numbers 24:14, Deuteronomy 4:30 and Deuteronomy 31:29. The alternate spelling of the "End of Days" appears in Daniel 12:13.

President Clinton announced the Camp David summit July 5, 2000, and Arafat and Barak began meeting with him July 11. My letter to Clinton was dated July 5, 2000.

Camp David ended in failure July 25. The new Intifada began September 29, after Ariel Sharon visited Temple Mount September 28. Sharon was elected Prime Minister of Israel February 6, 2001.

Rips confirmed the final results of his two-week computer run at Hebrew University May 1, 2001—the odds of the two Biblical expressions of the "End of Days" appearing with "Arafat" and "Barak" and "Sharon" and "Bush" were at least 500,000 to 1.

My sealed letter to my attorney Michael Kennedy was dated October 6, 1998.

"Shahid," the Arabic word for "suicide bomber," literally means "martyr" but is used by both Israelis and Arabs to describe the terrorists who blow themselves up in bomb attacks.

Dr. Rips confirmed that the odds against "World War" and "Atomic Holocaust" and "End of Days" all appearing with "in 5766" (2006) were at least 100,000 to 1 in a telephone conversation on May 17, 2001. "It might be higher," said Rips. "I only looked in 100,000 random texts, and none were better."

## CHAPTER TWO: CODE KEY

Exodus 24:10 states that Moses "saw the God of Israel and there was under his feet a kind of paved work of sapphire stone."

The legend that God wrote the original words of the Bible on "sapphire stone" is cited in Kaplan, *The Living Torah*, p. 379, and attributed to an ancient commentary on the Bible, *Sifri, BeHaAlothekha*, 101. See also Kaplan, p. 420.

Rabbi Adin Steinsaltz, the foremost translator of ancient Hebrew texts, told me when we met at his study in Jerusalem that Isaiah 41:23 states "to see the future you must look backwards," and that the same words in Hebrew said, "read the letters in reverse."

In May 1998, shortly before Shavuot, the holiday that celebrates the giving of Torah, I met with Rips in Jerusalem and showed him that his name (in Hebrew the reverse of Sapphire) appeared in the verse of the Bible that describes God coming down on Mount Sinai.

The quote that Rips read to me from the Genius of Vilna came from an English translation of *The Jewish Mind*, Abraham Rabinowitz (Hillel Press, 1978, pp. 33–34).

I finally found the obscure Hebrew word for "obelisks" in the definitive four-volume Hebrew dictionary *The New Dictionary*, by Abraham Even-Shoshan (Kiryat-Sefer Press, Jerusalem, Israel, 1985). The meaning of the word was also confirmed by ancient commentary on the Bible, called the Midrash.

The 1700-year-old Midrash that states the "obelisks" "were not what a human being had made, but the work of Heaven," is the *Mekhilta According to Rabbi Ishmael, An Analytical Translation* (trans. Jacob Neusner, Scholars Press, Atlanta, GA, 1988). The same text suggests the obelisks were humanoid, "a kind of male and female." See also Marcus Jastrow, *The Book of Words*, who calls the "obelisks" "cavernous rocks resembling human figures" (Judaica Press, New York, 1996, p. 460).

Rips's email confirming that "Code Key" twice crossed "Mouth of the Obelisks" against odds of a million to one was sent January 2, 2002. In a later telephone conversation, on January 6, Rips told me that "in the history of code research no other pair has had such high statistics."

"Mouth of the Obelisks" and "Lord of the Code" both appear in the plain text of the Bible as the names of locations in Egypt at the edge of the Red Sea, where the Pharaoh and his army overtook the fleeing Hebrew slaves.

But these two places, whose names are never translated in the Bible, whose plain open meaning in Hebrew was never recognized, could not be the location of the "code key," or of the "obelisks."

Moses did not receive the Bible on Mount Sinai until after the Hebrews had escaped Egypt. Therefore, the key to the Bible code could certainly not have been buried in Egypt.

And in the Bible code itself, the location of the "code key," of the "code on the obelisk" is very clearly stated—the "Valley of Siddim."

Genesis 14:3 states that "the Valley of Siddim is the Dead Sea." The most famous commentator on the Bible, the Rashi, states that the valley was once green but that long ago the Mediterranean Sea flowed into it, creating the Dead Sea (*Pentateuch with Targum Onkelos, Haphtaroth, and Rashi's Commentary*, trans. Rev. M. Rosenbaum and Dr. A. M. Silbermann, Jerusalem, 1929, p. 55).

I met with Israeli geologist David Neev at his home in Jerusalem in November 1998, and on several later occasions. He told me that the Dead Sea was now at its lowest level in more than 5000 years. Neev, the leading authority on that area, also told me that "Siddim" in Hebrew means "lime," and suggested that the Lisan Peninsula, which is covered by limestone, might be the last remaining aboveground remnant of the Valley of Siddim.

I first visited the Lisan in November 1998, and returned there in March and April 1999, first with two Israelis from the Geophysical Institute of Israel and then with two Jordanian geophysicists. On February 16, 2000 I went back to the Lisan with a Neev protégé, Yuval Bartov, a young Israeli geologist who is the leading expert on the Lisan, and Mikhail Rybakov, an Israeli geophysicist, accompanied by officials from the Jordanian Ministry of Tourism and Antiquities.

Two days earlier, on February 14, 2000, I met in Amman with Minister Akel Biltaji, and he assured me that we would get the necessary permits for the archaeological survey. The written permit dated April 13, 2000 was in fact granted by the Director of the Department of Antiquities, Dr. Fawwaz Al-Khraysheh.

It was solely the Bible code that led me first to the "Valley of Siddim," then to the Dead Sea, and finally to the exact spot on the 25-square-mile Lisan Peninsula. The code clearly described its most northern point, where a finger of land juts up into the Dead Sea, forming a small bay called Mazra, as the location of the "code key."

"Lisan as Siddim" appears in Daniel 1:4, and "Mazra" appears in Daniel 1:3, as part of an extended passage whose hidden text also describes a "pillar in the palace" inscribed with ancient wisdom, perhaps the "obelisk."

## CHAPTER THREE: CLINTON

President Clinton confessed his "relationship" with Monica Lewinsky August 17, 1998. On September 21, 1998 I sent *The New York Times* Op-Ed page a column with the Bible code's prediction that Clinton would survive the scandal. On February 12, 1999, the U.S. Senate acquitted Clinton on both articles of impeachment.

My letter to Clinton was dated July 5, 2000, the day he announced the Camp David summit. I sent it July 7, after his Chief of Staff Podesta agreed to give it to the President, with my first book about the Bible code. On July 17, the Chief of Staff's assistant called and stated, "Mr. Podesta gave your material directly to the President at Camp David."

The Camp David summit started July 11 and ended in failure July 25. Clinton publicly blamed Arafat, stating that Barak "moved forward more from his initial position than Chairman Arafat, particularly surrounding the question of Jerusalem," *The New York Times* reported July 26, 2000.

My first letter to Barak dated May 17, 1998, predicting that he would be Prime Minister, was sent to him through General Isaac Ben-Israel, chief scientist at the Ministry of Defense. A year to the day later, on May 17, 1999, Barak became Prime Minister.

I sent a new letter to Barak through Ben-Israel and his Cabinet Secretary Isaac Herzog the same day, noting that the code also predicted that

Barak would be Israel's leader "at a time of great danger," specifically involving Temple Mount.

"'They will strike Temple Mount' is just as clearly encoded with 'Prime Minister E. Barak' as the assassination was encoded with 'Yitzhak Rabin,'" my letter to Barak stated.

Ben-Israel had told me on May 29, 1998 in New York that Barak personally investigated the Bible code after Rabin was killed, when he was a Cabinet Minister.

*The New York Times Magazine* article about the danger of an attack on Temple Mount in the millennial year 2000, by Jeffrey Goldberg, was published October 3, 1999. It quoted Hamas leader Sheik Yassin as stating, "This will be the end of Israel."

My meeting with Abu Ala, the leader of the Palestinian Parliament, took place August 13, 2000, at his office in Ramallah.

On September 20, 2000 I sent a fax to Clinton's Chief of Staff Podesta: "Religion is the problem. The Bible code may be the solution." He agreed to see me at the White House October 16.

The new Intifada began September 29, 2000, after Friday prayers on Temple Mount. Four rock-throwing youths were killed by Israeli soldiers at the mosque, as reported in *The New York Times*, the Israeli press and on CNN. The day before, on September 28, the leader of Israel's right wing, Ariel Sharon, led 1000 riot police and soldiers onto Temple Mount, triggering the Palestinian uprising.

I met with Barak's brother-in-law, Doron Cohen, at his Tel Aviv law office October 12, 2000, and gave him a new letter for Barak. But while we were meeting he received news that two Israeli soldiers had been lynched at a police station in Ramallah. My description of the lynching is based on filmed reports broadcast on CNN and the BBC.

I met with Nabil Sha'ath in Gaza October 10, 2000, and gave him a letter for Arafat. Two days later, the compound we met in was destroyed by a missile fired from an Israeli helicopter.

On October 16, 2000, I met with Clinton's Chief of Staff Podesta at the White House. He told me he had already talked to the President about the Bible code, and said he would speak to him again.

Podesta told me that he could believe the Bible code was real, and said "Clinton is also religious." He promised to arrange a meeting with the President, but it never took place in Clinton's troubled last months of office.

## CHAPTER FOUR: IT EXISTS

In Hebrew, the name of the peninsula "Lisan" also means "language." Therefore, the full code matrix that runs parallel to "Bible code" states two different things: "It exists in Lisan," and "it exists in the language of man."

I spoke to Dr. Rips about that new finding July 11, 2000. My discovery was the result of a finding made by his computer programmer, Dr. Alex Rotenberg, who originally found the full spelling of "Bible code" with two very short skip sequences, against odds of 5000 to 1.

What is literally encoded is "Torah code," but throughout this book I refer to it by its more familiar form, "Bible code."

I saw Rips in Israel April 5, 2001, and we discovered together that "Bible code" is crossed by "dictionary" where "Lisan/language" appears twice. Rips discovered that the two verses of the Bible that deal most directly with "language," Genesis 10:5 and Genesis 11:6, appeared on the same table.

The Rosetta stone was found in 1799 near a town in northern Egypt at the mouth of the Nile. The stone had parallel inscriptions in Egyptian hieroglyphics and Greek, making it possible to decipher the ancient Egyptian picture writing.

Many scholars have suggested that there was a proto-language of all mankind. Charles Darwin, in 1871, said "man has an instinctive tendency to speak" (*Descent of Man*, John Murray, London). The linguist Noam

Chomsky first suggested that language has genetic roots more than 40 years ago. See *Language* 35, pp. 26–58 (1959). See also Luigi Luca Cavalli-Sforza, *Genes, Peoples, and Languages* (New York: North Point Press, 2000).

Rips, in claiming Hebrew was the original language, cites the best-known commentator on the Bible, the Rashi, who quotes Genesis 11:1— "And the whole Earth was of one language"—and states it was "the Holy Tongue (Hebrew)." *Pentateuch with Targum Onkelos, Haphtaroth, and Rashi's Commentary*, see above, p. 44.

*The New York Times* report that a "language gene" had been discovered was published October 4, 2001, citing an article in the journal *Nature*, Dr. Anthony P. Monaco.

No one knows how or when language began. Some scientists claim evidence for language in hominid skulls millions of years old, but others, like Stanford archaeologist Richard Klein, argue that a specific genetic change produced the modern human brain only 50,000 years ago, and made language possible. This follows Chomsky's 1959 theory that there is a dedicated language organ embedded in the brain's circuitry.

A later report, cited in the *Times* August 15, 2002, by Dr. Svante Paabo at the Max Planck Institute, states that a study of the genomes of humans and chimpanzees shows that language evolved only in the last 100,000 years. The Paabo paper was published in the journal *Nature*.

In the Bible code, "the language gene" is crossed by "God's gene" and the extended verse of the Torah states, "Before the lord destroyed Sodom and Gomorrah, it was like God's own garden" (Genesis 13:10). In Hebrew, the same letters that spell "language gene" also spell "Garden of Lisan," and "God's gene" also spells "God's garden."

The Jordanian newspaper *Al-Arab Al-Yawm* published a front-page attack on my foundation's archaeological expedition January 9, 2001.

Almost every statement in the newspaper story was untrue, but the basic message was clear: "Why would a Jewish foundation be allowed to dig for Jewish artifacts on Jordanian territory?"

I spoke to the American Ambassador in Amman, William J. Burns, January 24, and again after he sent me a translation of the newspaper story, January 28, 2001.

## CHAPTER FIVE: ARAFAT

My April 12, 2001 letter to Arafat was picked up from the American Colony Hotel in Jerusalem that midnight.

Arafat Chief of Staff Nabil Abu Rudaineh called me at 1:15 A.M. on April 13, 2001, asking me to come see Arafat that evening.

I met with Arafat at 9 P.M. on April 13 at his walled compound in Ramallah. Also present at our meeting was his chief negotiator, Saeb Erekat, who translated for us, and Rudaineh.

*The New York Times* reported July 23, 2000 that Arafat told Clinton he feared assassination if he gave up Jerusalem.

Nabil Sha'ath, Arafat's foreign minister, told me in a telephone conversation December 26, 2000 that Arafat believed a basic teaching of Islam— "our destiny is pre-ordained, and we do not have one day more, or one day less, to live. "

I met with Rips at his home in Jerusalem on the morning of the day I saw Arafat, April 13, 2001. Rips did not try to dissuade me from the meeting, but did compare Arafat to Hitler and Saddam Hussein.

When Arafat said that "Muhammad said we have one thousand years but not two thousand," he was stating a Muslim tradition not in the Koran, but in its commentary, the Hadith. In the Muslim calendar, 2001 was the year 1422, 400 plus years into the second millennium Muhammad said we would not survive. The Koran states that mankind cannot know the time of the end.

"Arafat" is spelled in the hidden text of the Bible just below "in the End of Days," exactly as his name is spelled in modern Israeli newspapers.

On the same code table, the names of the Israeli leaders "Barak" and

"Sharon" and the U.S. President "Bush" all also appear in the Bible code spelled as they are in the Israeli press.

The day I met with Arafat, Friday April 13, 2001, Christians, Jews and Muslims all converged on the Old City in Jerusalem—Christians to celebrate Good Friday and reenact the crucifixion on the *Via Dolorosa*, Jews to doven at the Wailing Wall, the remnant of the ancient Temple on the penultimate day of Passover, and Muslims to pray on their Sabbath at the mosque on Temple Mount above.

The coincidence of holy days only highlighted the religious conflict that had lasted thousands of years, and still centered on the battle for Jerusalem.

## CHAPTER SIX: STEEL ARK

"Steel" appears in Hebrew with "code key" in the Torah, and "iron" in Aramaic with "key today" in the Book of Daniel. Aramaic is an ancient Semitic language very similar to Hebrew, and half of Daniel is written in it.

"Iron furnace" appears in Deuteronomy 4:20, a text that is believed to be more than 3000 years old. The Hebrew word for "steel" comes from a later book of the Old Testament, one of the lesser prophets, Nahum 2:4— "the chariots glitter with steel." Nahum was written nearly a thousand years after the Torah.

"This is the solution," words spoken by the ancient prophet Joseph, appear twice in Genesis 40:12 and 40:18. The first verse crosses "steel ark" and the second crosses "iron ark." Both are overlapped in the hidden text by the name of the peninsula, "Lisan."

My meeting with Rips took place in Nashville, Tennessee, where he was a visiting professor at Vanderbilt University in January 2000.

The same Hebrew letters in Exodus 35:33, a verse about the artisan who built the tabernacle, also spell "forged iron, all the work of the computer."

The two verses of Joshua that mention an "iron vehicle" are 17:16 and 17:18. Both appear where "Tel of the Obelisks" is encoded.

When I returned to the Lisan on February 16, 2000 with a Jordanian archaeologist from the Department of Antiquities, Dr. Fawzi Zayadin, he questioned whether an iron or steel object could have survived thousands of years. An Israeli geophysicist who was with us, Mikhail Rybakov, said that even if some remnant of the object had survived, if it was rusted, it would not be seen by a magnetometer.

I interviewed Professor Ronald Latanision of MIT by telephone on February 25, 2000. A leading expert on corrosion, Latanision confirmed that an iron or steel object might survive for thousands of years, underground or underwater, in a very high salt environment.

"When you reach thirty-five percent salt in water the oxygen starts dropping very quickly," said Latanision. "Without oxygen, there is no rust."

This confirmed what the Israeli geologist David Neev had told me years earlier. I re-interviewed Neev, the leading authority on the Dead Sea area, March 6, 2000, and he confirmed that the concentration of salt in the Dead Sea was above 35 percent.

Neev also told me that he had seen engineers mining salt at the Dead Sea intentionally put iron pipes in the water to keep them from rusting.

MIT's Latanision also confirmed to me what a CIA scientist had said— that ancient steel from the Middle East was more likely to remain rust free than modern steel.

Latanision said that how the steel is hammered, and what impurities are hammered in, determines how long the steel will last, and that ancient steel swords were "more rust resistant than modern steel."

There are two different expressions for magnetometer in Hebrew. The more common spelling means, literally, "magnetic measuring instrument." The other form means, literally, "attraction sensor." The second is encoded with "iron" just above it in the plain text, and the other is encoded in the only place "detector" appears with no skips in the Bible.

The instrument can sense any iron-based object underground or underwater, up to a depth that is determined mainly by the size of the object.

If an ancient steel object is found, it will be possible to date it with great accuracy, using a newly discovered, little known method. A Yale geophysicist, Dr. Carl Turekien, told me June 1, 1999 that he and his Ph.D. student Nikolass VanderMurray, now a Harvard professor, found that carbon-14 dating works for all iron and steel made before the nineteenth century. Modern steel makers use coal, which has no radioactive carbon, and therefore can't be dated. But all older steel was made with charcoal from trees, and vegetable matter can be dated.

"The Lowest Place on Earth Is Subsiding," a report by Israeli geologist Gidon Baer, was published by the Geological Survey of Israel in November 2000. It reveals that the exact area of my search, the newly exposed land on the Lisan Peninsula, is sinking at a very fast rate.

On October 5, 2000, I flew to Amman, Jordan, to again see the American Ambassador, William Burns. It was the first week of the new Intifada, and when I arrived the American Embassy was surrounded by 20,000 angry demonstrators. I met with Burns October 8, and on the same day saw the Deputy Prime Minister of Jordan, Saleh Rusheidat.

## CHAPTER SEVEN: SHARON

I met with Omri Sharon, the Prime Minister's son, at the King David Hotel in Jerusalem on April 17, 2001.

The night before, mortar shells fired from Gaza landed in Israel just down the road from the Prime Minister's ranch. Israeli tanks and helicopter gunships immediately retaliated, invading Gaza, as reported in the Israeli newspapers *Ha'aretz* and *The Jerusalem Post* and in the *International Herald Tribune*.

All the Israeli press reported April 16 Omri's secret meetings with Arafat the week before, revealing that he had met with Arafat just two days before I did on April 13.

Sharon was elected Prime Minister February 6, 2001, which was 13 Shevat, 5761, in the Hebrew calendar. The date was encoded with "Sharon" and found months earlier, when all of Israel assumed former Prime Minister Benjamin Netanyahu would be the Likud candidate, and win the election.

The pre-election quotes from Sharon about the impossibility of making peace are from a January 29, 2001, *New Yorker* article by Jeffrey Goldberg, "Arafat's Gift," pp. 57, 67.

The letter for the Prime Minister I gave Omri was dated April 17, 2001.

I spoke to General Isaac Ben-Israel, chief scientist at the Ministry of Defense, April 1, 2001, and met with him at Israeli military headquarters in Tel Aviv April 12. He called General Meir Dagan, who had been chief of counter-intelligence in the Netanyahu administration, but was closer to Sharon than anyone aside from Omri.

I met with General Dagan in the town where he lived in northern Israel, Rosh Pina, April 4, 2001. He was quoted in *The Jerusalem Post* November 23, 2000, as telling an anti-peace rally in Jerusalem that "the time has come to send Yasir Arafat back to Tunisia."

Dagan told me he had read my first Bible code book when it was originally published in Hebrew in 1997, and that he took the warnings in the code seriously.

I gave Dagan a letter for the Prime Minister dated April 4, 2001, that he promised to give Sharon. But when they finally met April 16, Israel was in the midst of a crisis, and the Prime Minister only wanted to talk about his planned invasion of Gaza, following the mortar attack near his ranch, and another attack by Israeli jets on a Syrian radar station deep inside Lebanon.

"I saw him," Dagan told me the next morning, "but I did not give him your letter. I thought it would be a mistake in the midst of the crisis, without any explanation of the code."

I next saw Dagan in Jerusalem December 4, 2001. He had just been named to lead the Israeli team in cease-fire talk with the Palestinians, mediated by the U.S. envoy General Anthony Zinni.

Again Dagan promised to talk to Sharon on my behalf, but Israel was again in crisis, following three major suicide bombings that had killed twenty-five Israelis in the past few days.

On September 10, 2002 Sharon appointed Dagan Chief of the Mossad, as reported in *Ha'aretz* September 11, 2002.

I met with Israeli Foreign Minister Shimon Peres at his office in Tel Aviv April 22, 2001. I had last seen Peres when he was Prime Minister on January 26, 1996.

Peres was known to the world, and in Israel, as the architect of Oslo, of the peace plan that failed, but he had also been in charge of creating Israel's nuclear weapons at a top secret military base in Dimona, and understood the threat of nuclear terrorism. Three days after I first met with him in 1996, when he was Prime Minister, after I first told him the Bible code warned of an "atomic holocaust," Peres made a speech stating that the greatest danger facing the world was that nuclear weapons would "fall into the hands of irresponsible countries, and be carried on the shoulders of fanatics." On September 13, 2002, after a meeting at the White House, Peres predicted that the Middle East would become "either peaceful or nuclear" within five to ten years.

## CHAPTER EIGHT: CODE OF LIFE

I interviewed Francis Crick by telephone, October 27, 1998. He was at his office at the Salk Institute in San Diego, California. Crick won the Nobel Prize in 1962, with James Watson, for their discovery of the structure of DNA.

Dr. Crick first published his theory that "organisms were deliberately transmitted to the Earth by intelligent beings on another planet" in a scientific journal edited by the astronomer Carl Sagan, *Icarus*, Vol. 19, pp. 341–46, July 1973. He called his theory "Directed Panspermia."

Crick, both in our interview and in his original article, rejects similar theories that DNA arrived here in a meteorite, and instead stated that "a primitive form of life was deliberately planted on Earth by a technologically advanced society on another planet," using a "spaceship."

I met with Dr. Rips at his home in Jerusalem on November 27, 1998, exactly one month after Crick confirmed what the Bible code stated: "DNA was brought in a vehicle."

Rips agreed it was possible that both the Bible code and the code of life had the same double helix structure, two spirals intertwined, and showed me a code table he had found long before, where "judgment of God" was intertwined with "mercy of God."

It is not possible to truly show the structure of the Bible code on a two-dimensional printed page, or computer screen, because it is really a three-dimensional cylinder. As Rips explained, it is just like laying a map out flat instead of showing the globe.

Crick's further elaboration of his theory of Directed Panspermia is quoted from his book *Life Itself* (Simon & Schuster, New York, 1981).

In that book, Crick states, "The genetic code is the small dictionary which relates the four-letter language of the nucleic acids to the twenty-letter language of the proteins" (p. 171).

A fuller, more up-to-date explanation appears in *Genome* by Matt Ridley, which tells the story of the newly decoded human blueprint (Harper-Collins, New York, 2000). It also calls the genetic code a "language."

It is interesting that many ancient Creation myths, starting with the first known Sumerian writings, state that everything was called into existence with words, that by being named they were created.

As Dr. Rips told me, it is yet more explicit in Judaism: "The Torah came before the world—first God created the Torah, and then from it He created the universe." Again, it is the letters, the language, that is the blueprint of Creation.

## CHAPTER NINE: INVASION

The March 29, 2002, invasion of Ramallah, the storming of Arafat's compound in the West Bank city by Israeli tanks, was reported in *The New York Times*, *The International Herald Tribune*, and the Israeli newspaper *Ha'aretz*. My account is also based on CNN and BBC coverage of the siege.

Israel's invasion, its occupation of nearly every major city in the West Bank, followed a series of suicide bombings that peaked March 27, with a terrorist attack at a hotel Passover Seder in the coastal town of Netanya that killed nineteen and wounded more than one hundred.

The name of the Israeli military operation, "Defensive Wall," is encoded in the Bible exactly as it was spelled in the Israeli press, as are the names of the two cities where the heaviest fighting took place, "Jenin" and the "Casbah" section of Nablus.

I could not reach Omri Sharon, who was called up for military duty along with thousands of other Israelis. But I did meet again with General Dagan in Tel Aviv April 1, 2002, and showed him the remarkably accurate prediction in the Bible code of the current warfare. Dagan told me he had already given Prime Minister Sharon my letter from our last meeting, but I gave him a new letter dated April 1 for Sharon.

At Dagan's urging, Sharon's chief of staff Uri Shani agreed to meet with me, after a series of meetings between the Prime Minister and U.S. Secretary of State Colin Powell, who had just arrived in Israel to negotiate a cease-fire.

I met with Saeb Erekat, Arafat's chief peace negotiator, April 6, 2002, in Jericho, the only major West Bank city that Israel had not occupied. I gave him a new letter for Arafat dated April 6.

The quoted column in *The New York Times* by Thomas Friedman—stating that "weapons of mass destruction" might "wipe Israel off the map"—appeared March 10, 2002.

My meeting with Dalia Rabin, the daughter of the slain Prime Minister, took place at the Knesset December 3, 2001, on my prior trip to Israel. That same day, in a precursor to the March invasion, Sharon launched the biggest Israeli assault on the West Bank and Gaza since Rabin and Arafat shook hands on the Oslo accords in 1993.

Dalia Rabin quit her post as Deputy Defense Minister in July 2002, stating that Sharon had abandoned the effort to make peace.

I met with General Yossi Kuperwasser at the Kirya, Israeli military headquarters in Tel Aviv, on April 15, 2002. I told Kuperwasser, the chief intelligence analyst, the location of a possible terrorist base connected to bin Laden encoded in the Bible. Although the name of the location is very clearly stated in the code, I did not include it in this book for security reasons.

On September 4, 2002, Prime Minister Sharon said on Israeli television, "Libya is becoming perhaps a more dangerous country than we thought. Libya may be the first Arab country with weapons of mass destruction."

I did not know if it was my warning from the Bible code to General Kuperwasser that finally made its way to the Prime Minister, but it was at least confirmation of a consistent warning in the code.

I met with Dan Meridor, the Israeli Cabinet Minister who deals with chemical, biological, and nuclear terrorist threats, in his Jerusalem office April 9, 2002.

Meridor's September 11, 2001 statement—"Unfortunately, this attack is only the beginning"—was quoted in *Ha'aretz* October 22, 2001.

Israeli Defense Minister Benjamin Ben-Eliezer stated "Around 2005, Iran will have nuclear capabilities" in a January 2002 speech to the Council for Peace and Security, quoted in *Ha'aretz* January 11, 2002.

The CIA estimate that Iraq will build a nuclear weapon as soon as 2007 was quoted in *The New York Times* September 8, 2002.

Uri Shani quit as Sharon's chief of staff on April 18, 2002, ending any immediate chance for me to see the Prime Minister.

The statement by Israel's then-Prime Minister Levi Eshkol to the young general Sharon after the 1967 war—"the Arabs will still be here"—was quoted in the book *Six Days of War* by Michael Oren (Oxford University Press, New York, 2002).

Officially, only East Jerusalem and the Golan Heights in the north were "annexed" by Israel after the 1967 war, but Israel also at the same time occupied the West Bank and Gaza. In March 2002, for the first time since the peace accords in 1993, Israel re-occupied the West Bank, and in June 2002 re-invaded the territories.

In September 2002, after two years of the Intifada, at least 1790 Palestinians and 609 Israelis were dead, according to a *New York Times* report September 17, 2002.

I made a final effort to reach Prime Minister Sharon through his son Omri as this book was going to press in September 2002, and sent him the following email:

"OMRI: You ask, What can be accomplished? My answer, Israel can survive."

## CHAPTER TEN: ALIEN

SETI, the Search for Extra Terrestrial Intelligence, started in 1992 to search for radio signals from outer space, first as a U.S. government project, later as a privately funded program.

In 1999, the National Aeronautics and Space Administration named a Nobel Laureate, Dr. Baruch Blumberg, to head its newly formed Astrobiology Institute, aimed at detecting life beyond Earth. In June 2002, NASA announced it would launch spacecraft to probe the cosmos for extraterrestrial life, as reported in *The New York Times* June 4, 2002. According to the same *Times* report, there are now 85 known planets orbiting other stars.

When the first two planets outside our solar system were discovered, *Time* magazine ran a cover story, "Is Anybody Out There?," February 5, 1996. It reported, "Two American astronomers have found two planets outside our solar system whereon conditions exist that may be hospitable to life."

Australian physicist Paul Davies in his book *Are We Alone?* notes that the discovery of an alien radio signal would not lead rapidly to a dialogue between our civilizations: "A message from aliens 100 light years away would take 100 years to reach us, and any reply would take another 100 years to get back to them" (Basic Books, 1995, p. 42).

"There is an alternative scenario: The discovery of an alien artifact or message on or near the Earth," notes Davies, who suggests that it might be "programmed to manifest itself only when civilization on Earth crossed a certain threshold of advancement" (ibid).

Carl Sagan's suggestion that other intelligent life in the universe might have evolved far earlier, and therefore might be far more advanced, and that their technology might "seem to us like magic," is stated in his book *Pale Blue Dot* (Random House, 1994, p. 352). The author of *2001*, Arthur C. Clarke, made a similar observation: "Any sufficiently advanced technology is indistinguishable from magic," *Profiles of the Future* (Holt Rinehart & Winston, 1984).

The "Vision of the Chariot" quoted from the plain text of the Book of Ezekiel appears in Ezekiel 1:4–5. There is a similar passage in Daniel 7:9–10 about the "Ancient of Days" landing on Earth in a "throne" shooting fire: "A fiery stream issued and came forth from before him."

## CHAPTER ELEVEN: BUSH

My August 3, 2001 letter to President Bush was received by his Chief of Staff Andrew Card at the White House August 7, and according to his chief assistant Josephine Robinson, Card gave a copy to the President's National Security Advisor Condoleezza Rice. On September 10, 2001 I called to confirm that Bush had received the letter after he returned from his Texas vacation, and Ms. Robinson told me, "It was read by the two highest-ranking people here. But it is their decision not to give it to the President."

*Time* magazine reported May 27, 2002 that the CIA told the President

August 6, 2001 that bin Laden's followers might hijack airliners and that a month earlier an FBI report that never reached the President warned that bin Laden might be sending operatives to flight schools in America.

The suspected twentieth hijacker, Zacarias Moussaoui, was arrested August 16, 2001, but according to the *Time* report, the FBI failed to find a crucial clue on his computer, a name that would have led to the leader of the 9/11 attack, Mohammed Atta.

On August 28, 2002 *The New York Times* reported that a secret Senate report concluded that the government had a "veritable blueprint for 9/11 before the attack." And *The Washington Post* reported June 20, 2002 that the National Security Agency intercepted a message September 10, 2001 stating "Tomorrow is zero hour," but that the Arabic communication was not translated until September 12.

I sent a second letter to President Bush through Card and Rice October 1, 2001 noting that the September 11 attack was encoded in the Bible 3000 years ago, and again warning that, according to the code, World War III might start while Bush was in office. There was no response, although Bush himself believed that "September 11 confirmed that God had chosen him for a purpose, and showed him what that purpose is," according to a *New York Times* column by Bill Keller, March 23, 2002. There was a similar report in the *Times* September 22, 2001 stating that Bush told religious leaders in the White House that he had "encountered his reason for being"—September 11.

My account of the Bush/Gore election night conversations November 7, 2000 came from reports on NBC, ABC and CBS, and stories in *The New York Times* the next day.

The U.S. Supreme Court decision December 12, 2000 that halted the Florida recount, making Bush President, was broadcast on all the networks live, and reported in *The New York Times*.

Mohammad Atta's hand-written journal, found by the FBI after 9/11, made clear that he believed he was on a mission from God. "God, I trust in you," he wrote in Arabic, "God, I lay myself in your hands." And Atta instructed the other hijackers to pray when they entered the planes, "Oh God, open all doors for me."

The Bible code named a possible terrorist base in the Middle East that crossed both Hebrew spellings of "Bin Laden" against very high odds, and called the location his "army headquarters." The same location was clearly encoded with "atomic weapon," "atomic holocaust," "chemical attack," and "the next war." I gave that information to intelligence officials at a high level in both the American and Israeli governments. Israeli intelligence officials took the warning seriously, but I had no indication that the American officials did.

I also warned the Israelis and Americans that Libya, or a "Libyan weapon," might be used in some ultimate attack by terrorists. The Israeli newspaper *Ha'aretz* reported May 22, 2002 that "Libya's efforts to obtain nuclear weapons increasingly worry American and Israeli officials. The Libyan threat was discussed in a round of strategic talks between the two countries held last week in Washington."

I do not know if my warning from the Bible code led to the new focus on Libya, or if the Israelis and Americans just independently arrived at the same conclusion.

I tried to reach Deputy Secretary of Defense Paul Wolfowitz, who had strong ties to Israeli intelligence, February 19, 2002. My fax stated: "The base, if it exists, may be linked to Bin Laden, and may be a source of danger to the United States as well as Israel." Wolfowitz replied to me through his assistant Linton Wells March 19, and declined to meet with me.

I sent a letter dated May 19, 2001 to Secretary of State Colin Powell, telling him I had just met in April with Arafat and Peres. "Even if you cannot believe there is a code in the Bible that predicts the future," I wrote Powell, "it may still be important that we meet, because Arafat clearly does." Powell did not reply.

Vice President Cheney's statement that a new terrorist attack against the U.S. was "almost certain"—"not a matter of if, but when"—was quoted in *The New York Times* May 20, 2002. He made similar statements on NBC's *Meet the Press,* May 19.

Defense Secretary Donald Rumsfeld's statement that terrorists would obtain weapons of mass destruction was made in testimony May 21, 2002 in a hearing at the Senate Appropriations Committee. Rumsfeld repeated his warning the next day in an interview on PBS: "They're perfectly willing to kill thousands of innocent men, women and children by flying airplanes into buildings. We know that they wouldn't hesitate a second to use weapons of mass destruction, if they had them."

Tom Ridge, director of Homeland Security, stated in a *New York Times* interview September 6, 2002, "We are now, and will be in the foreseeable future, the target of a single or multiple terrorist attack."

FBI Director Robert Mueller's statement that further terrorist attacks were "inevitable" and "we will not be able to stop it" was quoted in *The New York Times* May 21, 2002. Mueller apparently did not know that his comments to a law enforcement conference would become public. Mueller admitted May 29 that the 9/11 attacks might have been prevented if scattered intelligence reports the government had before September 11 had been connected, according to a *New York Times* report May 30, 2002.

## CHAPTER TWELVE: HERO JOURNEY

Joseph Campbell's statement of the classic "Hero Journey" appears in his book *The Hero with a Thousand Faces* (Princeton University Press, 1968), p. 30. Campbell's statement that the godly powers "are revealed to have been within the heart of the hero all the time" appears on p. 39.

Moses' last words to the ancient Israelites appear in Deuteronomy 30:11–14. Dr. Rips's statement that the consistent encoding of "obelisk" and "code key" was beyond chance, but not proof that the objects exist in this world, was made when I met with him in January 2000, and we had similar discussions through the years.

Rips noted that in the plain text of the Bible, there was an open reference to a copy of the entire Torah carved on stones, and that ancient commentary said it was in fact carved onto stones in 70 different languages for all the nations on Earth.

"So it is not unthinkable that your 'obelisks' may exist," said Rips, "and of course I would be more than thrilled if you found them."

The story of Joseph being re-named by the Pharaoh "Zaphenath-Paneah"—which in Hebrew means "decoder of the code"—appears in Genesis 41:45. "This is the solution," words spoken by Joseph when he twice reveals the future, appear in Genesis 40:12 and 40:18. Both times, the name of the peninsula "Lisan" overlaps his statement.

Dr. Rips's statement that the code "comes from an intelligence that is not merely higher, but different" came at a meeting I had with him shortly before Passover in March 1999. In that same meeting, Rips told me that for the Encoder, there is no distinction between past, present, and future.

Einstein's similar statement—"The distinction between past, present and future is only an illusion, however persistent"—appears in a letter he wrote the widow of a fellow physicist and lifelong friend, Michele Besso, on March 21, 1955 (Einstein archive 7–245, published in *The Quotable Einstein*, Princeton University Press, 1996), p. 61.

I spoke with film director Stanley Kubrick about the Bible code on several occasions while I was working on my first book in the mid-1990s. When I first told him about the Bible code, Kubrick's immediate reaction was, "It's like the monolith in *2001*."

Stephen Hawking stated that "time travel might be within our capabilities" in his introduction to *The Physics of Star Trek* (Basic Books, 1995), p. xii. Hawking repeats his belief in time travel in the latest edition of his book *A Brief History of Time* (Bantam, 1996), p. 211. He also notes that any advanced form of space travel would require faster-than-light travel, which automatically means going back in time.

Bin Laden's statement—"Americans love life, that is their weakness. We love death, that is our strength"—was made in one of his taped appearances on the Arabic network Al-Jazeera, believed to have been recorded before 9/11, but broadcast later.

## CHAPTER THIRTEEN: COUNTDOWN

My statement to Rips in the days after 9/11 that even totally secular people now believe that we live in the End of Days was confirmed by a cover story in *Time* magazine July 1, 2002, "The Bible & the Apocalypse: Why more Americans are reading and talking about the End of the World." It quotes the senior minister of the staid Fifth Avenue Presbyterian Church in Manhattan: "Since Sept. 11, hard-core, crusty, cynical New York lawyers and stockbrokers who are not moved by anything are saying, 'Is the world going to end?'"

The prophecy of a "Final Battle" in the New Testament is quoted from the King James Version, Book of Revelation 20:7–9. The Old Testament quote—"Is this the man that made the Earth to tremble?"—is from the Book of Isaiah 14:16.

A time of terrible suffering before the coming of a Messiah is foretold in Chapter 12 of the Book of Daniel in the Old Testament, in Chapter 20 of the Book of Revelation in the New Testament, and in the commentary on the Koran called the Hadith.

The sealed letter I gave my attorney Michael Kennedy was dated October 6, 1998.

My letter to Alan Greenspan, the chairman of the Federal Reserve, was dated September 13, 2001, and delivered to Greenspan's office September 17. That happened to be the eve of the Hebrew New Year 5762 that was encoded with "economic crisis," and also the day the stock markets reopened for the first time since September 11. The Dow Jones fell 684 points, its biggest loss in history, beginning a week that saw the worst stock market crash since the Great Depression, according to a September 22, 2001 *New York Times* report.

Greenspan's press assistant Lynn Fox confirmed September 28, 2001 that the Chairman "read your letter," but never gave interviews, and would not meet. *The New York Times* reported November 27, 2001 that the National Bureau of Economic Research had officially declared a "recession."

In July 2002, the worst bear market in a generation sent all the major stock indexes back down below the depths they hit right after 9/11. *The New York Times* reported July 23, 2002 that the Dow had fallen below 8000 to 7702, its lowest close since October 1998, and the Standard & Poor's Index fell below 800 to 797, its lowest close since April 1997. The *Times* also reported July 21 that the market had lost $7 trillion in just two years.

The stock market ended the Hebrew year 5762 on Friday, September 6, 2002, with losses on six of the last eight trading days, and in each of the last five months, the first time the Dow had been down five months in a row since the 1981 recession. The *Times* reported on September 4, 2002 that the market "now looks likely to fall for three consecutive years, the longest stretch since the Depression."

The name of the terrorist base encoded in the Bible with "in the End of Days" is intentionally omitted. I gave the name of the location to both American and Israeli intelligence.

The Israeli newspaper *Ha'aretz* reported October 31, 2001 that "the most dangerous non-conventional threat that Israel faces today is smallpox, security advisors told Prime Minster Ariel Sharon."

According to Jonathan Tucker, *Scourge* (Atlantic Monthly Press, New York, 2001), smallpox claimed "hundreds of millions of lives" before it was eradicated from the world in 1980. His book also states that a third of its victims die and even most survivors are left with horrific effects. Both the U.S. and Israel decided in the summer of 2002 to vaccinate health-care and emergency workers, the frontline against any bioterrorist attack. The *Times* reported July 7, 2002 that the U.S. will vaccinate half a million health-care workers and that it now has 100 million doses of smallpox vaccine and by the end of 2002 will have enough for the entire American population. Israel, according to *Ha'aretz*, has already stockpiled enough vaccine for its entire population.

General Isaac Ben-Israel, chief scientist of the Ministry of Defense, told me December 12, 2001 that smallpox is "everyone's nightmare," because it spreads from person to person, it's airborne, and in today's world it would be global within weeks. "It's very easy to do," said Ben-Israel, "and it would be criminal to ignore."

My quote from my first Bible code book, published in 1997—"nuclear terrorists may trigger the next World War"—appears on p. 130 (*The Bible Code*, Simon & Schuster, New York, 1997).

The U.S. Senate report on the danger of nuclear terrorism, "Global Proliferation of Weapons of Mass Destruction" (Sen. Hrg. 104–422), was published in 1995. The quote re: the fall of the Soviet Union—"never before has an empire disintegrated while in possession of 30,000 nuclear weapons"—is from the opening statement of Senator Sam Nunn, transcribed October 31, 1995.

*The New York Times Magazine* cover story about nuclear terrorism by Bill Keller was published May 26, 2002. It stated in a bold headline, "SOONER OR LATER, AN ATTACK WILL HAPPEN HERE." The computer model of the impact of a 1-kiloton nuclear device exploded in Times Square quoted by Keller was developed by Matthew McKinzie, a scientist at the Natural Resources Defense Council. My description is quoted from Keller's article.

The descriptions of the impact of a 1-megaton bomb dropped on New York are quoted from Jonathan Schell's definitive book *The Fate of the Earth* (Knopf, New York, 1982) pp. 47–49. Schell's account of the likely impact of a 20-megaton bomb is quoted from pp. 52–53. His description of a ground-burst attack is quoted from p. 53.

Terrorism expert Robert Wright wrote in his *Times* op-ed column September 24, 2001 of 9/11—"the terrorists did not use biological or nuclear weapons, and next time they well could."

Dr. Rips's quotation of Moses' warning of "the evil that will befall you in the End of Days" is from Deuteronomy 31:29. He noted that the extended passage of Moses' last words makes clear that we have a choice, and ends with the statement, "Through this word you shall prolong your days on the Earth."

## CODA

Newton's statement that not only the Bible but the entire universe is a "cryptogram set by the Almighty" is stated by John Maynard Keynes in "Newton, the Man" (*Essays and Sketches in Biography*, Meridian Books, 1956).

The human genome was deciphered by two teams of scientists, one government and one private, and jointly announced June 26, 2000 and reported in *The New York Times* June 27 with the headline "GENETIC CODE OF HUMAN LIFE IS CRACKED BY SCIENTISTS."

The Hubble Space Telescope is sending back images that come ever closer to capturing light from the beginning of the universe. "The farther telescopes can see, the older the light they are viewing—up to 13 billion years past, approaching what scientists believe to be the dawn of time," *The New York Times* reported July 23, 2002.

British Astronomer Royal Sir Martin Rees states that a few numbers imprinted at the moment of Creation determined the shape of everything in his book *Just Six Numbers* (Basic Books, 2000) p. x.

Newton believed that the universe was a puzzle God made, that we were meant to solve. Dr. Rips believes that the Bible code is a puzzle God made, and the code itself states it is "in our hands to solve."

# APPENDIX

By discovering and proving the existence of a code in the Bible that reveals events that took place thousands of years after the Bible was written, Eliyahu Rips has challenged modern science and changed the way we see the world.

"If this is real, then it's a more important discovery than Einstein's," Israel's most respected physicist, Yakir Aharonov, told me when I first told him about the Bible code years ago.

"If this is real, then it's as important a discovery as Newton's," Aharonov said when I again met with him recently.

"You've upgraded it," I said. "Yes," said Aharonov. "If it's real, it will transform science the way Newton did."

But as Thomas S. Kuhn points out in his classic book, *The Structure of Scientific Revolutions*, many of the greatest discoveries are rejected, and even ridiculed, by the scientific establishment—specifically because all great discoveries, by definition, challenge what we think we know, and therefore challenge the scientific establishment.

"Each of them necessitated the rejection of one time-honored scientific theory in favor of another incompatible with it," wrote Kuhn. "Normal science often suppresses fundamental novelties, because they are necessarily subversive."

I remember warning Eli Rips before my first book about the Bible code was published that when his discovery became known on a large scale he would be attacked. It was inevitable. He was asking the world to accept a theory so radical that once it was accepted the world would never be the same.

"You're challenging the world the way Galileo did when he said that the Earth circled the Sun, that the Sun, not the Earth, was the center of our world. It wasn't just the Church that condemned him; it was also the entire scientific establishment of his day. You also are challenging both the religious establishment and the scientific establishment."

"I'm only happy they no longer burn people at the stake," said Rips.

But Rips was to face a different kind of ordeal. He was attacked by many ordinary scientists who could not accept that a phenomenon they couldn't understand might be real.

Yet no one could find a flaw in the math or the computer science of his original experiment, the experiment Rips published in August 1994 in a respected peer-reviewed U.S. mathematics journal, *Statistical Science*. No one even submitted a rebuttal.

Then, five years later, *Statistical Science*, under a new editor, did publish a rebuttal, written by a team of mathematicians led by an Australian who did not read the language of the Bible code, Hebrew.

However, he had a number of Israeli allies who challenged neither the math nor the computer science of the original Rips experiment, but instead attacked the data —the list of Hebrew names of the 32 sages, all of whom lived after the Bible was written but whose dates of birth and death remarkably matched their names in the Bible code.

The same phenomenon could be found in any book, said the critics. It was the first question I had asked Rips, when we first met. Couldn't the same apparent coincidence be found in any book, using a computer?

Rips told me that he and his colleagues had in fact looked for the same names and the same dates, using the same computer program and the same mathematical test in three other non-Biblical texts.

In the Bible, the names and dates were encoded together. In the three other books they were not. And the odds of finding the encoded information by random chance were ultimately found to be 1 in 10 million.

"The data was fitted to the test," claimed the critics. The rebuttal stopped just short of accusing Dr. Rips and his colleagues of fraud, of picking names and dates that would match only in the Bible.

I knew that was untrue, because I had checked out the facts before I published my first book. It was the second question I asked Rips—who chose the data?

In fact, the names of the sages were chosen mechanically. Rips and his colleagues simply measured the column inches for the entries in the *Encyclopedia of Sages*, the one standard reference work, and chose first the 34 who had at least x inches. When the scientist supervising the original experiment asked for fresh data—specifically to rule out any possibility of fraud—Rips chose instead the next 32 sages whose entries in the encyclopedia were at least x inches long.

There was no possibility of manipulation. The choice of the names was purely mechanical.

But there was some dispute over the proper spelling of the names of these rabbis, most of whom lived in a time before spelling was consistent and standardized. So Rips and his colleagues asked the leading authority on rabbinical bibliography, Professor Shlomo Z. Havlin, to independently decide the proper spellings, and thereby make the final choice of the data for their experiment. I interviewed Havlin, and he also gave me a written statement:

"I have confirmed that each of the two lists of names and denominations were decided by my judgment, and that I scrupulously examined this against the computerized databank of the Data Processing Center of Bar-Ilan University."

Before *Statistical Science* published its five-year-late rebuttal, Havlin sent the journal an even more detailed statement of his role in deciding the data used in the original Rips experiment:

"I must emphasize that, in the course of preparing the above-mentioned lists, not only was it impossible for me to know what effect the choice of a particular name or appellation would have on the success of the experiment, I also had no idea how the success of the experiment would be gauged, and in which way it was connected to the list of names and appellations."

The original Rips experiment was a classic double-blind experiment. The independent expert who chose the data did not even know how the data would affect the outcome of the experiment. Indeed he had no knowledge of the experiment at all.

The basic accusation against Rips and his colleagues—that they "fitted the data to the test"—was obviously not true. Neither Rips nor his two colleagues who performed the experiment with him chose the data. Havlin did.

But although *Statistical Science* was informed, in writing, in advance, by Havlin that the accusation against Rips was untrue, the rebuttal was nonetheless published.

The rebuttal included one other challenge to the Rips experiment. The Australian Brendan McKay did his own "experiment," not in the Bible but in *War and Peace*. And in it, he admittedly manipulated the data to create a fake "code" in the Russian novel.

The point he was trying to make was that if he could rig an experiment, fake a "code," then Rips also could have done that.

Of course, the claim was both silly and untrue. First of all, Rips could not have rigged his experiment because an independent expert, Havlin, chose the data. And Havlin didn't know how the data would affect the outcome.

But beyond that, all McKay had proven was that he had faked an experiment, that he had perpetrated a hoax. As the most famous mathematician in Israel, Robert Aumann at Hebrew University, commented, "If McKay had counterfeited a hundred-dollar bill, that would not prove that all money was fake. It would only prove that McKay was a counterfeiter."

The challenge was so clearly untrue, and so clearly absurd, that under ordinary circumstances it never would have been published.

But in fact it was embraced by many scientists because they had already made up their minds. What Rips stated, what he had proven, what no one could prove wrong—that there was a code in the Bible that revealed events that took place after the Bible was written—so completely challenged modern Western science that some Western scientists decided without examining the evidence that it could not be true.

If Rips was right, they were wrong. If Rips was right, the laws of physics, mathematics, the nature of time itself had to be reexamined.

It is the same challenge that has confronted nearly every scientist who has made a great discovery, any discovery that challenged the science of their own day.

But to this day, no one has found any evidence that Rips is wrong. No one has challenged his math, or his computer science, or the outcome of his original experiment, which showed that the names of 32 sages who lived after the Bible was written matched the dates of their births and deaths against odds of 10 million to 1.

In fact, a senior code-breaker at the U.S. National Security Agency, Harold Gans, replicated the Israeli experiment using his own computer program. Gans was so certain that the Bible code could not be real that he then took his experiment a step further—he looked in the code for new information, the names of the cities where the same sages were born and died. He found them, encoded in the same place.

McKay et al. falsely claim in their attack on Rips that Gans had "withdrawn" his experiment. In fact, Gans publicly stated in writing that he had reconfirmed his experiment and was certain of its results.

"Our most telling evidence against the 'codes' is that we cannot find them," wrote McKay et al., ignoring the fact that a 25-year veteran of NSA, who spent his life making and breaking codes for American military intelligence, did find a code in the Bible.

Moreover, McKay et al. twice, in fact, themselves found clear evidence that the Bible code was real. First they challenged the original selection of names, claiming the column inches in the *Encyclopedia of Sages* were not accurately measured. When the original Rips experiment was redone using the data McKay selected, the result was actually better. McKay et al. ignored that experiment.

Then, in their own first experiment, seeking to debunk the Bible code, McKay et al. actually found a positive result. Instead of reporting it, they changed their experimental method, setting new parameters Rips warned them in advance precluded the possibility of a positive result. They then published the results of that second experiment, hiding in the new data the positive results of their first experiment.

And, of course, no one has explained how the Bible code could accurately predict the future if in fact it is not real. No one has found in *War and Peace* or *Moby Dick* a correct prediction, in advance, of a world event.

No one could manipulate a false code to accurately predict a year in advance the assassination of a Prime Minister.

Perhaps that is why nearly everyone outside of a small circle of scientists accepts the reality of the Bible code.

In its attack, *Statistical Science* noted that Rips's "paper was reprinted in full in the book of Drosnin (1997) that has been a best-seller in many languages, so it is possibly the most printed scientific paper of all time."

Yet the Rips paper has drawn only the one obviously false rebuttal in any scientific journal.

In his reply to *Statistical Science* Rips and his colleagues showed by detailed mathematical analysis that McKay's challenge had "no validity whatsoever." Rips also noted that "the statements of the esteemed scholar Prof. S. Z. Havlin of Bar-Ilan University, and Harold Gans, who was a senior code-breaker at the U.S. Department of Defense, clearly show the falsity of its accusations."

"The evidence for the Bible Code is stronger than ever," wrote Rips. "Startling progress has been achieved, which includes new experiments that show that both characters in the Bible, and people who lived long after the Bible was written, are named and encoded with the details of their lives."

But the math journal that originally published Rips's experiment, and promised in writing to allow him to reply to any rebuttal, refused to publish his reply.

The most respected mathematician in Israel, Aumann, who is also a member of the American Academy of Sciences, sent a written protest to *Statistical Science* that was also signed by one of the best known mathematicians at Harvard, David Kazhdan, objecting to the journal's refusal to allow Rips and his colleagues to reply to the attack.

"We are acutely aware of the explosive nature of the original article," Aumann and Kazhdan wrote. "*Statistical Science* is to be warmly congratulated for having the intellectual honesty and courage to publish it despite the storm it was bound to—and did—create."

Aumann cautioned *Statistical Science* not to follow its original brave publication with "shoddy, inappropriate and inequitable procedures," and specifically not to publish a rebuttal written in secret, and never even shown to Rips.

But the math journal ignored the letters of Havlin, Gans, Aumann and Kazhdan, and published a paper that had been rebutted in advance.

I am certain that the paper Rips originally published will one day be seen as a "scientific revolution."

# ACKNOWLEDGMENTS

This new book began when I found the name of the Israeli mathematician who discovered the Bible code in a verse of the Bible that tells of God coming down on Mount Sinai to give Moses the Torah.

In the five years since then, we have spoken often, and met many times. The evidence that the Bible code is real came from many sources, but this book could not have been written without Eli Rips's constant help.

It was written independently of him, however, and the views expressed in it are mine, not his, except for his quoted remarks.

I used the computer program he created with his colleague Dr. Alex Rotenberg. All the Bible code printouts were made using software Alex created with Dr. Alex Polishuk.

Many Israeli government officials helped in important ways. I won't thank them all by name, because that might make their jobs more difficult, but I must thank my friend General Isaac Ben-Israel, who was until recently the chief scientist at the Ministry of Defense. Also, Joel Singer, the lawyer who wrote the Oslo peace accords and helped me reach important people in Israel and Jordan.

Two geologists, David Neev and his young protégé Yuval Bartov, shared their knowledge about the Dead Sea and the Lisan, making my archaeological search possible.

Several friends took time to read, criticize, and encourage. One, Jon Larsen, did far more. His advice has been both bold and intelligent, and he's encouraged me often through the years.

Two other friends, my attorneys Ken Burrows and Michael Kennedy, helped in ways that went far beyond legal advice. My agent, John Brockman, managed to keep this book a secret while orchestrating simultaneous worldwide publication.

Wendy Wolf, my editor at Viking, made a difficult job easy, and managed to bring this book out in record time. Susan Petersen Kennedy and David Shanks, the President and the CEO of Penguin Putnam Inc., were enthusiastic from day one, and gave me total support. I must also thank Jaye Zimet, the design director, and Chip Kidd, who created the jacket.

The book would not have been possible without the help of my two assistants, Diana and Talya. Diana kept everything in order, found the unfindable, and did important research. Talya, a brilliant young Israeli, not only confirmed the translations, but also helped me write the book. I would not have made it without her.

# INDEX